BEYOND TRADITION

BUILDING FUTURE ON YOUR TERMS

SATYAM TYAGI

To the trailblazers and pioneers,
Who dares to challenge the status quo,
And carve their path through the wilderness of tradition,
This book is lovingly dedicated to you.

In a world where conformity often reigns supreme,
You stand as beacons of individuality and courage,
Fearlessly embracing your uniqueness,
And refusing to be bound by the chains of expectation.

To those who believe in the transformative power of choice,
Who understands that true freedom lies in authenticity,
And who recognizes that the road less traveled
Is often the one that leads to the most profound discoveries,

This book is a testament to your unwavering spirit,
Your relentless pursuit of truth and self-discovery,
And your unyielding commitment to building a future
That reflects the fullness of your dreams and aspirations.

May these pages serve as a source of inspiration,
A reservoir of wisdom, and a wellspring of hope,
As you navigate the twists and turns of your journey,
Forging ahead with unwavering determination and grace.

Contents

Foreword

In a world inundated with norms and expectations, the journey of self-discovery can often feel like navigating a labyrinth of tradition and convention. It is amidst this labyrinth that "Beyond Tradition: Building Future on Your Terms" emerges as a guiding light, offering a roadmap to those who dare to defy the status quo and carve their path.

In these pages, you will embark on a transformative journey—one that challenges conventional wisdom, questions societal norms, and celebrates the beauty of individuality. From redefining the institution of marriage to nurturing authentic relationships, from navigating the complexities of education and career to mastering the art of personal finance, this book is a comprehensive guide to building a life that reflects your deepest values and aspirations.

As you delve into the chapters that follow, I invite you to approach each topic with an open mind and a courageous spirit. Embrace the discomfort of challenging ingrained beliefs, for it is through this discomfort that true growth and liberation are often found. May the insights shared within these pages inspire you to embrace your uniqueness, empower you to make informed choices, and embolden you to craft a future that is authentically yours.

To the seekers, the dreamers, and the architects of their own destiny—this book is for you. May it serve as a beacon of hope and inspiration on your journey toward a life lived on your own terms.

Warm regards,
Satyam Tyagi

Preface

Welcome to "Beyond Tradition: Building Future on Your Terms." This book is born out of a deep-seated belief in the power of individual agency and the transformative potential of choice. In a world where societal norms often dictate the trajectory of our lives, it is easy to lose sight of our desires and aspirations amidst the clamor of external expectations.

The genesis of this book lies in my own journey of self-discovery—a journey marked by moments of doubt, introspection, and ultimately, liberation. Through personal experiences and conversations with individuals from all walks of life, I have come to realize that the path to fulfillment lies not in conforming to predefined roles, but in embracing our authentic selves and making choices that resonate with our deepest values.

"Beyond Tradition" is more than just a book—it is a call to action, a manifesto for those who refuse to be confined by the limitations of tradition and convention. It is a testament to the boundless potential that lies within each of us, waiting to be unleashed through the power of choice and self-determination.

In the pages that follow, you will find a treasure trove of insights, reflections, and practical advice on navigating the complexities of modern life. From reimagining the institution of marriage to charting your course in education and career, from nurturing meaningful relationships to mastering the art of personal finance, this book offers a comprehensive roadmap to building a life that is uniquely yours.

As you embark on this journey, I encourage you to approach each chapter with an open mind and a sense of curiosity. Allow yourself to question long-held beliefs, challenge societal norms, and explore new possibilities. For it is in the process of questioning and exploration that true growth and transformation occur.

I am deeply grateful to all those who have contributed to the creation of this book—whether through their insights, their stories, or their unwavering support. Each story in this book is purely fictional. It is my sincere hope that "Beyond Tradition" will serve as a source of inspiration, empowerment, and guidance as you embark on your own journey of self-discovery and personal fulfillment.

With warmest regards,
Satyam Tyagi

Acknowledgements

Writing a book is never a solitary endeavor; it is the culmination of countless moments of inspiration, support, and encouragement from those around us. As I reflect on the journey that led to the creation of "Beyond Tradition: Building Future on Your Terms," I am filled with gratitude for the many individuals who have played a role in bringing this vision to life.

First and foremost, I would like to express my heartfelt appreciation to my family and friends, whose unwavering belief in the importance of this project provided the foundation upon which this book was built. Your guidance, wisdom, and encouragement have been invaluable throughout every stage of the writing process.

I am deeply grateful to the individuals who generously shared their insights, experiences, and stories, lending depth and authenticity to the pages of this book. Your willingness to open your hearts and minds has enriched the narrative in ways that words alone cannot express.

To my friends and family, who stood by me with unwavering support and understanding, I extend my deepest gratitude. Your love, encouragement, and patience sustained me through the highs and lows of the creative process, reminding me of the importance of connection and community.

I would also like to thank the countless mentors, colleagues, and collaborators who have contributed their expertise and perspective to this project. Your guidance and feedback have been instrumental in shaping the ideas presented in this book, and I am truly grateful for your generosity and insight.

Finally, I extend my sincerest thanks to the readers who will embark on this journey with me. It is my hope that "Beyond Tradition" will inspire you, empower you, and guide you as you navigate the complexities of modern life and chart your own course toward a future that is authentically yours.

With deepest gratitude,
Satyam Tyagi

Prologue

In the hushed moments before dawn, when the world is cloaked in shadow and silence, there exists a space where the boundaries of tradition begin to blur and the possibilities of the future stretch out before us like an open road. It is in this liminal space—the space between what was and what could be—that the seeds of change are sown, and the journey of self-discovery begins.

"Beyond Tradition: Building Future on Your Terms" invites you to step into this space of possibility, to challenge the constraints of convention, and to embrace the infinite potential that lies within each of us. It is a journey of exploration and transformation, guided by the belief that the choices we make today have the power to shape the course of our lives tomorrow.

In the pages that follow, we embark on a voyage of discovery—a voyage that takes us beyond the familiar shores of tradition and into the uncharted waters of personal freedom and empowerment. From reimagining the institution of marriage to navigating the complexities of education and career, from nurturing meaningful relationships to mastering the art of personal finance, this book is a compass to guide you on your journey toward a life that is uniquely yours.

But this journey is not just about charting a new course; it is about reclaiming the power to define our own destinies and shape our own future. It is about recognizing that the path to fulfillment lies not in conforming to the expectations of others, but in embracing our authentic selves and making choices that align with our deepest values and aspirations.

As we set sail on this voyage of self-discovery, I invite you to cast off the shackles of convention, to embrace the unknown with courage and curiosity, and to chart a course toward a future that is filled with possibility and promise. For it is in the journey itself that we discover the true meaning of freedom, and it is in the act of choosing that we begin to realize the limitless potential that lies within each of us.

So let us embark on this journey together, with open hearts and open minds, ready to explore, to learn, and to grow. For the journey of a lifetime awaits, and the adventure of self-discovery begins here.

Disclaimer

"*Beyond tradition doesn't mean just upgrading for the sake of change, but rather upgrading with necessary, positive, or healthy elements.*"

1

Empowering Education

Education is the key to unlock your full potential. We discuss the importance of lifelong learning, and exploring different paths to knowledge and personal growth.

Education is more than just a means to acquire knowledge; it is the key that unlocks the door to limitless possibilities. In a world where the landscape of learning is constantly evolving, empowering education takes on a new significance—one that goes beyond textbooks and classrooms to embrace the full spectrum of human potential.

Education stands as the cornerstone of human progress, a beacon illuminating the path to enlightenment and empowerment. Yet, in today's fast-paced and ever-changing world, the concept of education extends far beyond the confines of traditional classrooms and standardized tests. It encompasses a holistic approach to learning—one that nurtures not only the mind but also the spirit, fostering creativity, critical thinking, and a lifelong thirst for knowledge.

In the realm of empowering education, we delve deep into the heart of learning, exploring innovative pedagogies, transformative teaching practices, and the myriad ways in which education can catalyze personal and societal change. From the grassroots initiatives that are revolutionizing access to education in underserved communities to cutting-edge research reshaping our understanding of how we learn, empowering education is about equipping individuals with the tools, skills, and mindset they need to navigate an increasingly complex and interconnected world.

At its core, empowering education is about more than just acquiring information—it is about cultivating a deep-seated sense of curiosity, resilience, and agency. It is about empowering individuals to think critically, solve problems creatively, and embrace the opportunities and challenges of the 21st century with confidence and courage. Together, let us reimagine the future of learning, and build a world where every individual has the opportunity to unleash their full potential and contribute to the collective betterment of society.

*"Education is the most powerful weapon which you can use to change the world. - **Nelson Mandela**"*

Necessary Steps For Empowering Education:

Empowering education involves taking several necessary steps to ensure that every individual has access to quality education that fosters personal development, and critical thinking, and prepares them for future challenges.

- **Universal Access:** Ensure equitable access to education for all, regardless of gender, socioeconomic status, ethnicity, or geographical location. This may involve investing in infrastructure, providing transportation, and eliminating barriers such as school fees.
- **Quality Teachers:** Recruit and retain qualified and motivated teachers who are well-trained and supported. Continuous professional development opportunities should be provided to enhance teaching quality and effectiveness.
- **Curriculum Reform:** Update and diversify the curriculum to be inclusive, relevant, and responsive to the needs of diverse learners. This includes integrating practical skills, critical thinking, digital literacy, and global citizenship into the curriculum.
- **Safe and Inclusive Learning Environments:** Create safe, supportive, and inclusive school environments that promote respect, tolerance, and diversity. Measures should be in place to prevent discrimination, bullying, and violence.
- **Community Engagement:** Foster partnerships with parents, communities, and local stakeholders to support educational initiatives, raise awareness about the importance of education, and encourage participation in children's learning.
- **Resource Allocation:** Allocate sufficient resources, including funding, materials, and technology, to support effective teaching and learning.

- **Life Skills Education:** Integrate life skills education into the curriculum to equip students with essential skills such as communication, decision-making, problem-solving, and financial literacy.
- **Monitoring and Evaluation:** Establish robust monitoring and evaluation systems to assess educational outcomes, identify areas for improvement, and ensure accountability at all levels of the education system.
- **Promote Gender Equality:** Address gender disparities in education by promoting girls' enrollment and retention, providing support for menstrual hygiene management, and combating harmful gender stereotypes.
- **Merit-Based Evaluation:** Removing reservation from exams promotes a fair and merit-based evaluation system where candidates are judged solely on their capabilities, skills, and knowledge. It ensures that the most deserving candidates have equal opportunities to succeed.
- **Lifelong Learning Opportunities:** Promote lifelong learning opportunities for individuals of all ages through adult education programs, vocational training, and skills development initiatives that respond to changing economic and technological landscapes.

By implementing these steps, societies can empower individuals through education, enabling them to reach their full potential, contribute to sustainable development, and build inclusive and resilient communities.

Empowering Education: The Role of NGOs in Transforming Learning

Education NGOs play a crucial role in complementing government efforts and addressing gaps in the education sector. Here are some key aspects of their work and impact:

- **Advocacy and Awareness:** NGOs advocate for the right to education and raise awareness about educational issues, including access, quality, and equity. They engage in policy dialogue, lobby for reforms, and mobilize public support for education.
- **Program Implementation:** NGOs design and implement educational programs that cater to marginalized and underserved communities. These programs may focus on literacy, numeracy, vocational skills, or specific needs such as girls' education or children with disabilities.

- **Capacity Building:** NGOs build the capacity of local educators and communities through training programs, workshops, and resource sharing. They empower teachers with innovative teaching methods, curriculum development, and leadership skills.
- **Community Engagement:** NGOs work closely with communities to understand their educational needs and priorities. They promote parental involvement, establish community learning centers, and foster partnerships with local stakeholders.
- **Monitoring and Evaluation:** NGOs conduct monitoring and evaluation to assess the impact of their programs, improve effectiveness, and ensure accountability. They use data to inform decision-making and advocate for evidence-based policies.
- **Research and Innovation:** NGOs contribute to educational research, pilot innovative approaches, and share best practices. They leverage technology and digital platforms to enhance learning outcomes and reach remote or disadvantaged populations.
- **Resource Mobilization:** NGOs mobilize resources from donors, foundations, and corporate partners to sustain their educational initiatives. They manage funds efficiently, ensuring transparency and accountability in financial management.
- **Collaboration with Government and Partners:** NGOs collaborate with government agencies, other NGOs, academic institutions, and international organizations to leverage expertise, resources, and networks for greater impact.
- **Emergency Response and Resilience:** In crises such as conflicts, natural disasters, or pandemics, NGOs provide emergency education, psychosocial support, and resilience-building programs to ensure continuity of learning and support for affected communities.

Overall, education NGOs play a pivotal role in promoting inclusive and quality education, empowering individuals and communities, and contributing to sustainable development goals globally.

The Journey of Rajesh: From Job to NGO Founder:

Rajesh, a software engineer in a bustling city, found himself increasingly dissatisfied with the routine of his corporate job. Despite his success in the tech industry, he felt a deep-seated desire to contribute more meaningfully to society, especially to help underprivileged children who lacked access to education.

One day, on his way home from work, Rajesh noticed a group of children gathered around a street vendor, curiously trying to read the alphabet on a signboard. Seeing their eagerness to learn amidst their difficult circumstances struck a chord in Rajesh's heart.

Determined to make a difference, Rajesh began volunteering his evenings at a nearby slum, teaching basic literacy and math to the children there. Initially, he faced challenges in gaining their trust and maintaining their interest, but his patience and dedication soon paid off. The children began to eagerly await his lessons, and their progress became a source of immense joy for Rajesh.

As word spread about Rajesh's efforts, more parents in the community approached him, expressing gratitude and sharing stories of how their children's confidence and academic performance had improved. Inspired by their enthusiasm and driven by a sense of purpose, Rajesh decided to take a bold step—he quit his job to focus entirely on educating these children.

With the support of friends and family, Rajesh formally established an NGO called "Bright Futures Foundation." The organization aimed to provide quality education and holistic development opportunities to underprivileged children across the city. Rajesh tirelessly fundraised, recruited passionate educators, and expanded the NGO's reach to serve more communities in need.

Over the years, "The Bright Futures Foundation" grew into a reputable organization known for its innovative teaching methods, personalized mentorship, and impactful community projects. Rajesh's journey from a corporate job to an NGO founder not only transformed his own life but also touched the lives of countless children, offering them hope, education, and a brighter future.

Rajesh's story continues to inspire others to follow their passion and make a meaningful impact, proving that one person's dedication and compassion can indeed change the world.

"Always try to share your knowledge with your juniors and teach those children who can't afford education."

Nurturing Education at Home:

In a bustling suburban home, Maya and Rahul found themselves faced with the challenge of supporting their children, Aryan and Diya, through their academic journeys. As the school year progressed, they noticed Aryan becoming increasingly frustrated with his grades, especially in mathematics, while Diya struggled with concentration during study sessions.

Determined to foster a positive learning environment at home, Maya and Rahul began implementing structured routines and supportive strategies. They set aside dedicated study hours each evening, creating a quiet space free from distractions where Aryan and Diya could focus on their assignments and review lessons.

Recognizing the importance of emotional support, Maya and Rahul encouraged open communication with their children about their academic challenges. They listened attentively to Aryan's frustrations and Diya's difficulties, offering encouragement and constructive feedback. Instead of focusing solely on grades, they emphasized the value of effort, perseverance, and continuous learning.

To enhance their children's understanding of challenging subjects like mathematics, Maya and Rahul sought creative ways to make learning enjoyable. They used educational games, practical applications, and real-life examples to illustrate mathematical concepts, turning study sessions into interactive and engaging experiences.

Moreover, Maya and Rahul celebrated their children's progress and milestones, whether big or small, reinforcing a sense of achievement and motivation. They encouraged Aryan and Diya to set realistic goals and guided time management and study techniques to help them succeed.

Through their concerted efforts, Maya and Rahul not only created a supportive educational environment at home but also nurtured resilience, self-confidence, and a love for learning in Aryan and Diya. Their approach emphasized holistic development, ensuring that their children could navigate academic challenges with confidence and determination.

Handling Low Marks with Love and Understanding:

Academic setbacks, such as receiving low marks, can be disheartening for students and stressful for parents. Navigating these moments with love and understanding is crucial in fostering a supportive environment that encourages growth and resilience.

"When children receive low marks, it's crucial not to scold them but to explain with love. No matter how many times they get low marks,

approaching them with patience and empathy fosters a positive learning environment. This approach helps children understand their mistakes, encourages them to learn from them, and builds their confidence to do better in the future. Ultimately, nurturing their self-esteem and growth mindset is key to their academic and personal development."

Harnessing Technology for Meaningful Learning and Growth

Using technology and the internet for educational purposes or to learn something valuable is highly beneficial. It allows individuals to access vast amounts of information, connect with experts globally, and participate in online courses that enhance knowledge and skills. This use of technology promotes meaningful learning experiences and personal growth, rather than wasting time on vulgar content or idle entertainment. It empowers individuals to make productive use of their time and leverage technology for constructive purposes.

The Smartphone and the Journey to Success:

In a modest household, there was only one smartphone shared among family members. Each day, someone would listen to music, another would watch movies, and it seemed there was never enough time for everyone to use it. One day, the youngest son spoke up, "You can use the phone all day long, but please leave me just one hour after I return from college."

In that precious hour, he began taking online courses and soon found himself tutoring others with the knowledge he gained. His dedication paid off, leading to a job placement at a prestigious company.

Through discipline and determination, he transformed a shared device into a tool for personal growth and success, proving that with focused effort, even limited resources can lead to boundless opportunities.

The Value of Academic Books in Gaining Deep Knowledge:

In today's educational landscape, there is a growing belief that practical experience outweighs academic study. Many advocate focusing solely on practical knowledge, often dismissing academic books as outdated or less relevant. This perspective overlooks the crucial role that academic books play in providing a comprehensive and in-depth understanding of subjects.

Academic books are the result of years of dedicated research and scholarship. They offer detailed insights and core concepts that are not always captured in classroom notes or quick online summaries. While it is common for students to rely on notes or videos for exam preparation, these resources typically highlight only the essentials needed to pass tests, often omitting the nuanced understanding provided in academic texts.

The depth of knowledge contained in academic books goes beyond the surface-level information presented in notes. These books are meticulously crafted to cover the subject matter extensively, offering a profound comprehension of core principles that short summaries or videos cannot match. Reading academic books allows students to grasp fundamental concepts and theories, laying a strong foundation for both practical application and further academic exploration.

It is important to approach academic books with the understanding that they are more than just supplementary materials—they are essential resources for developing a thorough and informed perspective on any topic. By engaging with these texts, students can gain a more profound and nuanced understanding of their subjects, which is crucial for both academic and professional growth.

Ultimately, while practical experience is invaluable, it should complement, not replace, the knowledge gained from academic books. For a deep and well-rounded understanding of any subject, students should prioritize reading and studying these comprehensive resources, rather than relying solely on condensed notes or brief online content.

*"The best way to not feel hopeless is to get up and do something. Don't wait for good things to happen to you. If you go out and make some good things happen, you will fill the world with hope, you will fill yourself with hope. - **Barack Obama**"*

2

Crafting Your Career

Crafting Your Career emphasizes the art of not just pursuing professional success but also ensuring that it aligns with personal fulfillment and happiness. It encourages individuals to navigate their career paths with intentionality, considering factors beyond monetary gains or societal expectations. This approach advocates for a balanced life where career choices are made in harmony with personal values, relationships, and well-being, aiming for a holistic and satisfying journey toward professional achievement. Below are some points that can help you advance your career.

- **Personal Values and Career Choices**: Understanding your values—such as integrity, creativity, or helping others—and aligning them with your career choices ensures that your work feels meaningful and fulfilling.
- **Work-Life Balance:** Maintaining a healthy balance between work responsibilities and personal life commitments is essential for overall well-being, productivity, and sustained career success.
- **Professional Growth:** Continuous learning and skill development are crucial for staying relevant in your field, advancing your career, and seizing new growth opportunities.
- **Entrepreneurship vs. Employment:** Comparing the advantages and challenges of being an entrepreneur (creating your own business) versus being employed (working for someone else), helping individuals decide which path aligns best with their goals and aspirations.
- **Networking and Relationships:** Building and nurturing professional relationships through networking, mentorship, and collaborations can open doors to new career opportunities, insights, and support.

- **Career Transitions:** Strategies and considerations for successfully navigating career transitions, whether moving to a new industry, role, or level of responsibility, and managing the associated challenges and opportunities.
- **Impact and Legacy:** Exploring how to shape your career to make a positive impact on your community or industry, leaving a meaningful legacy that aligns with your values and aspirations.

After reviewing these, individuals can develop a robust framework to carefully plan and navigate their career paths, ensuring that achieving professional success is accompanied by personal fulfillment and growth.

Balancing Success and Happiness:

In today's world, the pursuit of a successful career is often portrayed as the ultimate goal. Society, educational institutions, and even family members emphasize the importance of securing a high-paying job, climbing the corporate ladder, and achieving professional recognition. While building a career is undoubtedly important, it's essential to recognize that a fulfilling life is composed of more than just professional achievements.

Meet Arjun, a young man who had always been driven by the desire to excel in his career. He graduated from a prestigious university and landed a job at a top-tier company. Arjun worked long hours, often sacrificing his weekends and personal time to meet deadlines and impress his superiors. His hard work paid off as he quickly moved up the ranks, earning promotions and accolades.

However, as Arjun's professional life flourished, his personal life began to suffer. He missed family gatherings, lost touch with friends, and neglected his health. His parents, who had always supported his ambitions, started to worry about his well-being. They noticed that despite his professional success, Arjun seemed increasingly stressed and unhappy.

One evening, Arjun's father sat him down for a heartfelt conversation. He reminded Arjun that while a successful career is valuable, it should not come at the cost of personal happiness and relationships. He shared stories of friends who had prioritized their careers over everything else, only to regret it later when they realized they had missed out on life's precious moments.

Arjun's father's words struck a chord. He began to reflect on his life and the choices he had made. He realized that his relentless pursuit of career success had led him to neglect the people and activities that brought him joy. Arjun decided it was time to make a change.

He started by setting boundaries at work, ensuring that he had time for himself and his loved ones. He rekindled old friendships, spent quality time with his parents, and took up hobbies he had long abandoned. Arjun also explored new career opportunities that allowed for a better work-life balance. He discovered that it was possible to have a fulfilling career without sacrificing his well-being.

Arjun's story highlights an important lesson: while crafting a successful career is important, it should not overshadow other aspects of life. True fulfillment comes from balancing professional aspirations with personal happiness. It involves nurturing relationships, taking care of one's health, and making time for activities that bring joy and relaxation.

In essence, a career is just one part of a larger puzzle. To craft a truly fulfilling life, it's essential to pay attention to all the pieces and ensure they fit together harmoniously. By doing so, we can achieve a sense of balance and contentment that no amount of professional success can replace.

Prioritizing Career and Professional Development During College:

During college, Maya found herself torn between enjoying the social aspects of student life and focusing on her career and professional development. Many of her friends spent their days attending parties and social events, while Maya dedicated her evenings to internships, workshops, and building her professional network.

Initially, Maya's approach seemed unconventional to her peers. They often questioned why she was so focused on career-related activities instead of fully enjoying her college years. However, Maya remained steadfast in her belief that laying a strong foundation for her future career was paramount.

As graduation approached, Maya's diligence began to pay off. She secured a coveted internship at a renowned company, which eventually led to a full-time job offer upon graduation. Her proactive approach during college had not only prepared her with valuable skills and experiences but also opened doors to promising career opportunities. Meanwhile, her friends are still grappling with career opportunities.

Reflecting on her journey, Maya realized that while college offered ample opportunities for personal growth and social experiences, prioritizing career and professional development had been crucial in shaping her future. She encouraged her peers to consider the long-term benefits of investing time and effort into building their careers early on, emphasizing that the skills and networks gained during college could significantly impact their post-graduation success.

Maya's story serves as a reminder to college students everywhere: while enjoying the college experience is important, dedicating attention to career and professional development can lay a solid groundwork for future success and fulfillment.

Upholding Integrity in a Sensationalized World:

In today's times, we often see on social media and elsewhere that people are becoming famous by engaging in vulgar activities. They don't even care about the quality of their content; they simply create it for the sake of becoming famous. But do they deserve respect? NO. That's why it's always important to do work that earns respect in society and never to compromise your standards. However, people on social media or so-called influencers often fail to understand this. They just create sensationalized content to gain views or go viral. It's your responsibility to choose the kind of content you consume. For example, many people follow YouTube controversies even though they have no relevance to their lives. Many students idolize educational startups and get caught up in their controversies, losing focus on their studies and ultimately failing as a result.

"In a scenario, there was an education startup 'BeforeA' that prepared students for academics and placements, earning their admiration and respect. Gradually, the startup became highly successful. Later, another startup 'AfterB' emerged with similar courses, gaining popularity among students who started preferring it. 'AfterB' aimed to offer affordable courses, claiming to prioritize students' welfare with the slogan "we think only for children" and continued in this way. 'AfterB' slowly started surpassing 'BeforeA'. However, controversy arose between the two startups when 'AfterB' began hiring teachers from 'BeforeA' with higher salaries. This led to students getting involved in controversies on social media, where insults were exchanged instead of focusing on their studies. In this situation, 'AfterB' gained more sympathy because of its affordable courses, and emotional connection with the students. Now, the question arises whether it was justified for 'AfterB' founders, who claimed to care for students and provide affordable education, to dismiss teachers from 'BeforeA', causing losses

to thousands of students. No, it wasn't justified. Therefore, the point here is that whether it's education or anything else, businesses must operate, despite claims of serving society on social media. Ultimately, everyone has their business interests, and due to a lack of understanding, students often suffer losses. People always price things cheaply and expensively according to their business. Therefore, students should carefully consider their decisions and choose their mentors wisely."

Choosing Hard Work Over Shortcuts:

It means opting to put in the necessary effort, time, and dedication to achieve a goal or complete a task, rather than seeking quick and easy ways that might compromise the quality or integrity of the outcome. It emphasizes the value of persistence, diligence, and the long-term benefits of genuine effort over immediate but potentially unreliable gains.

In the bustling city of Mumbai, Aryan, a young aspiring actor, faced the daunting challenge of breaking into the competitive film industry. Tempted by promises of quick fame and fortune, some of his peers resorted to sensationalism and controversy to gain attention. However, Aryan remained steadfast in his belief that genuine success could only be achieved through hard work and dedication.

While his friends chased viral stunts and scandalous publicity, Aryan focused on honing his craft. He attended acting workshops, studied classic films, and tirelessly auditioned for roles. His days were long and filled with rejection, but he persisted, knowing that true fulfillment came from mastering his skills rather than seeking fleeting popularity.

Months turned into years, and Aryan's perseverance began to pay off. He landed a supporting role in a critically acclaimed indie film, followed by a breakthrough lead role in a prestigious production. His performances garnered praise for their depth and authenticity, earning him a growing fan base and industry respect.

Reflecting on his journey, Aryan realized that while shortcuts might offer temporary success, they often came at the cost of integrity and long-term growth. By choosing hard work over sensationalism, he not only achieved his career goals but also earned genuine admiration and respect from peers and audiences alike.

Aryan's story serves as a reminder that genuine success is built on dedication, persistence, and a commitment to excellence. In a world often seduced by shortcuts and instant gratification, choosing the path of hard work not only leads to professional achievements but also fosters personal fulfillment and lasting impact.

*"You can only become truly accomplished at something you love. Don't make money your goal. Instead, pursue the things you love doing, and then do them so well that people can't take their eyes off you. - **Maya Angelou**"*

Don't Be Nice to Everyone:

"Don't Be Nice to Everyone" suggests that indiscriminate kindness can sometimes be detrimental. It encourages thoughtful consideration of boundaries and personal values when interacting with others. This approach promotes healthier relationships based on mutual respect and genuine connections rather than superficial niceties.

Asserting Boundaries in Professional Relationships:

Sarah, a marketing executive at a large corporation, was known for her friendly and approachable demeanor. She often found herself saying "yes" to every request that came her way, whether it was taking on extra projects or agreeing to work late hours to accommodate her colleagues' schedules. Initially, Sarah's willingness to help garnered praise and appreciation from her team.

However, over time, Sarah began to feel overwhelmed and stressed. She noticed that despite her efforts, some colleagues took advantage of her willingness to please, often delegating tasks to her without considering her workload or personal commitments. This pattern not only affected Sarah's productivity but also strained her relationships with colleagues, as she began to feel resentful and exhausted.

Reflecting on her situation, Sarah realized that her indiscriminate kindness was not serving her well. She decided to assert boundaries by prioritizing her tasks and politely declining additional work that exceeded her capacity. Initially, this shift was met with surprise and even some resistance from colleagues accustomed to relying on her constant availability.

However, as Sarah continued to maintain her boundaries with consistency and clarity, she noticed a positive change. Her colleagues began to respect her time and workload more, and they started to value her contributions based on the quality of her work rather than her availability. By being selective in how she extended her kindness and setting clear boundaries, Sarah not only regained her sense of balance and well-being but also cultivated healthier and more respectful professional relationships.

This example demonstrates how applying the principle of "Don't Be Nice to Everyone" in professional settings can lead to greater effectiveness, respect, and personal fulfillment. It underscores the importance of assertiveness and self-care in maintaining healthy boundaries while fostering genuine and productive interactions with others.

3
The Power of Friendship

Friendship is a bond that transcends time and circumstance. We celebrate the joys of companionship, exploring the transformative impact of true friendship on our lives and well-being. Friendship is crucial for emotional well-being, providing support, companionship, and a sense of belonging. Good friends offer comfort during tough times, celebrate successes, and enhance life with shared experiences. They help us grow, improve our self-confidence, and contribute to our overall happiness and mental health. In essence, friendship enriches our lives and fosters a strong, supportive community.

Role of Friendship in Mental Health and Well-being:

Friendship plays a crucial role in mental health and overall well-being. Having supportive friends provides emotional support, reduces stress, and fosters a sense of belonging. Close friendships can act as a buffer against mental health issues such as depression and anxiety by offering companionship and understanding during tough times.

Friends also encourage positive behaviors and can help individuals adopt healthier lifestyles by promoting physical activity, healthy eating, and adherence to medical advice. The social interaction provided by friends boosts mood and self-esteem, contributing to greater life satisfaction.

Additionally, friendships offer opportunities for personal growth and development. Through interactions with friends, individuals learn important social skills, gain new perspectives, and develop empathy. This social support network is essential for maintaining mental health and enhancing resilience, helping individuals navigate the challenges and stresses of life more effectively.

Be Attuned to Your Friend's Mental State:

Always strive to understand your friend's mental state, as they might need your support at any moment but may not express it. Friends can be upset over various issues like careers, higher studies, or relationships. Proactively checking in on them can make a significant difference. Encourage them by reminding them that life goes on despite challenges and that their happiness is paramount. Your attentiveness and understanding can provide the reassurance and comfort they need to navigate difficult times.

> *"John and Alex had been friends since childhood, sharing everything from laughter to dreams of a bright future. However, as life's pressures mounted, John struggled silently with stress and anxiety. One day, overwhelmed by his inner turmoil, John tragically chose to end his life.*
>
> *Alex was devastated. Guilt-ridden and heartbroken, he realized he hadn't been there for John when he needed him most. He hadn't noticed the signs or reached out in time. For months, Alex couldn't bear to speak about John, haunted by thoughts of how he could have made a difference.*
>
> *In time, Alex found solace in memories of their friendship. He vowed to never again ignore the struggles of those he cared about. Through his grief, Alex learned the profound lesson that reaching out and showing genuine concern can save a life, reminding everyone of the importance of supporting friends through their darkest moments."*

Value Your Friend's Dreams:

The idea of "Value Your Friend's Dreams" emphasizes the importance of mutual support and empathy in friendships.

- **Mutual Respect:** Respecting your friend's dreams and aspirations shows that you value their desires and ambitions just as much as yours.
- **Active Listening:** Listening actively to your friend's goals and providing support can strengthen your bond. It fosters a deeper connection and understanding.

- **Balanced Conversations:** Ensure conversations are balanced. If one person dominates the conversation with their own goals, it can make the other feel undervalued or ignored.
- **Encouragement:** Encouragement and constructive feedback on your friend's dreams can help them feel motivated and supported in their endeavors.
- **Reciprocity:** Friendships thrive on reciprocity. By showing interest in your friend's dreams, you're building a foundation for mutual support where both parties feel valued and heard.

Overall, this principle is about creating a supportive and balanced dynamic where both friends feel their dreams and goals are appreciated and respected.

Constructive Feedback for Friend's Success:

True friendship involves more than just agreeing with everything your friend says or does. Instead of simply nodding along, provide honest and constructive feedback to help them identify and overcome their shortcomings. By pointing out areas for improvement, you help them recognize their weaknesses and work on them. This approach fosters genuine development and stronger relationships. Instead of always saying "yes" to their ideas, providing honest and supportive critiques can lead to meaningful progress and mutual respect. True friendship involves guiding each other toward betterment and success through honest communication and encouragement. This approach fosters personal growth and success, as genuine friends challenge each other to be better and achieve their full potential. Constructive criticism, when given with kindness and respect, strengthens the friendship and contributes to mutual development.

Respecting Boundaries in Friendship:

It's not necessary to always go out with your friends for the friendship to thrive. If one friend doesn't feel like going out, they should be able to decline honestly. Friendships should have enough space for individual preferences and boundaries to be respected. If a friend refuses to go somewhere, this decision should be respected, not seen as a reason to end the friendship. True friendship is about understanding and honoring each other's choices, ensuring that both friends feel comfortable and valued.

Friendship is built on mutual respect, understanding, and trust. A crucial aspect of maintaining a healthy and lasting friendship is respecting each other's boundaries. Here are some key points to consider:

- **Communication:** Open and honest communication is vital. Friends should feel comfortable expressing their feelings and preferences without fear of judgment. If one friend doesn't want to participate in an activity, they should be able to communicate this freely.
- **Understanding:** It's important to understand that everyone has different comfort levels and boundaries. What one person enjoys might not be appealing to another. Recognizing and accepting these differences is essential for a healthy friendship.
- **Flexibility:** Friendships should be flexible enough to accommodate each other's needs. If one friend declines an invitation, it shouldn't be taken personally. Instead, find alternative activities that both can enjoy or respect their need for personal time.
- **Support:** True friends support each other's decisions, even if they don't always align with their desires. Showing support for a friend's choice to stay in or do something different reinforces the strength of the friendship.
- **Space:** Giving each other space is crucial. Being too demanding or expecting constant togetherness can strain the relationship. Allowing each other time to pursue individual interests helps maintain a healthy balance.
- **Empathy:** Put yourself in your friend's shoes. Understanding their perspective and respecting their wishes fosters a deeper connection and mutual respect.
- **Compromise:** Sometimes, compromise is necessary. Finding a middle ground where both friends feel comfortable can strengthen the bond and show that both parties are willing to make an effort.
- **Long-term Perspective:** Remember that friendships are long-term relationships. A single disagreement or differing preference shouldn't overshadow the entire relationship. Respecting boundaries ensures the friendship remains strong and resilient over time.

By respecting boundaries, friends can maintain a healthy, supportive, and enduring relationship. This approach not only preserves the friendship but also enhances the trust and respect that form its foundation.

A New Friendship Blossoms:

Once upon a time, there were two boys, Jack and Ryan, who attended the same tuition class. Ryan had been attending the tuition for quite some time, while Jack had just joined recently. The next day, Jack discovered that Ryan also attended his school but was in a different section. The following day, they met again at tuition but didn't speak to each other.

After school the next day, Jack noticed Ryan standing by the school gate, seemingly waiting for someone. Their eyes met, and Ryan walked over to Jack, saying he had been waiting for him. Jack was a bit shocked since they had only met two days ago and barely knew each other's names. Nonetheless, they shook hands and started walking together.

As they chatted, they arrived at Jack's house, and Jack invited Ryan inside. Ryan politely declined, saying it wasn't the right time. They continued meeting daily at tuition and school, and their friendship grew stronger. The next year, they ended up in the same section and began sitting together, although neither had visited the other's home yet.

Jack was academically stronger than Ryan, earning the nickname "Topper" from their classmates. Ryan was genuinely happy whenever their classmates called Jack "Topper," showing his support and pride in his friend's achievements.

As time passed, Jack and Ryan went to different colleges but made it a point to meet at Jack's house on weekends or once a month. They didn't communicate much through calls or chats, yet people admired how they maintained their friendship. Despite their different career paths, they respectfully discussed each other's pursuits and valued each other's opinions, which prevented any fights between them. They did have long debates on various topics, but these were always healthy conversations.

"Nowadays, there's a trend where friends insult each other, don't prioritize or listen to one another, and only talk about themselves before moving on. This kind of behavior eventually ends friendships. However, true friendship involves a special feeling that needs to be nurtured and protected, setting it apart from these negative trends. Whether a friendship is between boys or girls, certain factors are crucial for its longevity. These factors have helped Jack and Ryan maintain their strong bond without any complaints. This is why it's

said that best friends are often found unexpectedly, just like how Ryan began waiting for Jack the day after they met at tuition. Their friendship grew so deep that even their families became involved."

Heartwarming Approach to Friendship: A Lifelong Bond:

In a quaint neighborhood, two inseparable friends, Maya and Raj, shared a bond that transcended time and distance. From their childhood adventures of climbing trees to navigating the complexities of adulthood, Maya and Raj's friendship remained steadfast and unwavering.

Their friendship blossomed amidst shared laughter, heartfelt conversations, and mutual support through life's triumphs and tribulations. Maya, known for her infectious optimism, always had a knack for lifting Raj's spirits during moments of doubt or hardship. Raj, in turn, offered unwavering loyalty and a listening ear whenever Maya needed guidance or reassurance.

Their bond deepened over the years, marked by milestones such as celebrating each other's successes, comforting each other during setbacks, and cherishing moments of joy and laughter that only true friends understand. Despite living in different cities as adults, Maya and Raj made it a point to stay connected through regular phone calls, surprise visits, and heartfelt letters.

Their friendship was not just a source of companionship but a sanctuary of understanding and unconditional support. Whether sharing secrets over cups of coffee or embarking on spontaneous road trips, Maya and Raj cherished every moment spent together, knowing that their bond would endure the tests of time.

Through their story, Maya and Raj exemplify the heartwarming essence of true friendship—a relationship enriched by empathy, laughter, shared memories, and an unwavering commitment to each other's happiness and well-being.

"Friendship is born at that moment when one person says to another, 'What! You too? I thought I was the only one. - **C.S. Lewis**"

4
Cultivating Relationships

Cultivating relationships is about building and maintaining meaningful connections with others. It involves genuine communication, mutual respect, and empathy. In both personal and professional settings, strong relationships are founded on trust, understanding, and support. By actively listening, showing appreciation, and being dependable, you foster an environment where relationships can thrive. Over time, these connections can lead to collaboration, opportunities, and a richer, more fulfilling life. Cultivating relationships is not just about expanding your network, but about nurturing bonds that are mutually beneficial and lasting.

Importance of Trust and Honesty:

Trust and honesty are the cornerstones of any strong relationship. Being transparent and reliable in your interactions helps to build a solid foundation of trust. When people know they can count on you, it strengthens the bond and encourages open communication.

Active Listening and Empathy:

Active listening and empathy are crucial in understanding and responding to the needs and feelings of others. By genuinely paying attention and showing empathy, you demonstrate that you value and respect the other person's perspective, which strengthens the relationship.

Consistent Communication:

Regular and meaningful communication is essential in maintaining relationships. Whether it's through face-to-face conversations, phone calls, or messages, staying in touch helps keep the connection alive and shows that you care.

Mutual Respect and Appreciation:

Acknowledging and appreciating the contributions and qualities of others fosters a positive and supportive environment. Mutual respect encourages collaboration and the sharing of ideas, making relationships more rewarding.

Overcoming Challenges Together:

Facing challenges and conflicts is inevitable in any relationship. How you handle these situations can either strengthen or weaken your bond. Approaching difficulties with a collaborative mindset, patience, and a willingness to compromise can help overcome obstacles and build a stronger connection.

Shared Experiences and Memories:

Creating shared experiences and memories helps to solidify relationships. Whether through joint projects, social activities, or simply spending quality time together, these moments create a sense of belonging and shared history.

Supporting Each Other's Growth:

Encouraging and supporting each other's personal and professional growth is a vital aspect of cultivating relationships. By being a source of motivation and encouragement, you help each other achieve goals and reach new heights, enriching the relationship.

Building a Network of Relationships:

Cultivating relationships extends beyond individual connections. Building a network of relationships, whether in your personal life or professional sphere, creates a supportive community. This network can provide diverse perspectives, resources, and opportunities.

Investing Time and Effort:

Like any worthwhile endeavor, relationships require time and effort. Consistently investing in your relationships, whether through small gestures or significant acts, shows commitment and helps maintain the strength of your bonds.

"*Undoubtedly, many of you have journeyed from school to college, and during this time, a significant number of students—around 70-80%—tend to focus on their romantic lives rather than their studies. They often find excuses to befriend members of the opposite gender, developing these friendships into romantic relationships. These students soon start discussing marriage plans, such as how to convince their families, where to get married, and what to wear for the wedding. However, this preoccupation with their love lives leads to a decline in their academic performance, resulting in wasted tuition fees and lost opportunities.*

Some students, even as early as seventh or eighth grade, start seeking life partners, which can severely impact their career prospects. They engage in activities like lying to their parents to go to restaurants, watching movies, or skipping classes to hang out. This behavior leads to missed lectures and a lack of proper education, which ultimately hampers their future career prospects. Remember, finding a job doesn't necessarily mean their career is set, especially if they've missed critical learning opportunities due to distractions.

Over time, as they move to new classes, schools, or colleges, their preferences for partners change. When breakups occur, they face emotional breakdowns, health issues, missed studies, and poor academic results. Despite these consequences, they often don't consider the impact on themselves or their parents. Many times, they are deceived by their partners or mutually decide to seek new relationships, primarily because they lack the maturity to understand the dynamics of a committed relationship.

Ideally, if you find someone you like, you should communicate openly and make a mutual decision to spend time together. Once you are mature, graduate from college, or start your job or career, you can then ask your friend if they are willing to take the relationship to the next step. By then, you will have known each other for several years, fostering a deep understanding that can support a strong, lasting relationship. This approach ensures that you prioritize your education and career while building a solid foundation for your future together. Otherwise, you risk getting stuck in a cycle of unproductive relationships that hinder your progress."

A Lifelong Friendship that Shows Cultivating Relationship:

John and Sarah met in the first grade, and their friendship began with a shared love for drawing during recess. From that moment, they were inseparable, spending countless hours together both in and out of school. As they grew older, their bond only deepened, built on a foundation of trust, honesty, and mutual respect.

In high school, John faced a difficult period when his father passed away suddenly. Sarah was there for him every step of the way, offering a shoulder to cry on and a listening ear. She helped him navigate his grief, standing by him through the toughest days. John often said that he couldn't have made it through that time without Sarah's unwavering support.

After high school, they went to different colleges but made it a point to stay in touch. They called each other weekly, visited during holidays, and shared their dreams and fears. Their consistent communication kept their friendship strong, despite the physical distance.

Years later, Sarah was diagnosed with a rare illness. This time, it was John who provided the support. He would drive for hours to be by her side during treatments, bring her favorite books and meals, and ensure she felt loved and cared for. John's presence gave Sarah the strength to keep fighting, and she often said that his support was a crucial part of her recovery.

Their relationship wasn't just about supporting each other through hard times; they celebrated each other's achievements with equal fervor. When John published his first novel, Sarah was his loudest cheerleader. When Sarah completed her PhD, John was there in the front row, beaming with pride.

Their friendship also extended into supporting each other's families. When Sarah got married, John was her maid of honor. When John became a father, Sarah was named the godmother to his first child. Their families intertwined, creating a larger network of love and support.

Even as they grew older, John and Sarah continued to nurture their bond. They organized annual trips, ensuring they always had new shared experiences and memories. They supported each other's growth, both personally and professionally, celebrating milestones and offering advice during setbacks.

Their story is a testament to the power of cultivating relationships. Through trust, consistent communication, empathy, and mutual respect, John and Sarah built a lifelong friendship that not only enriched their own lives but also touched the lives of those around them. Their journey together shows that true relationships, when nurtured with love and dedication, can stand the test of time and be a source of immense strength and joy.

The Story of Two Generations: Grandfather and Grandson:

The Story of Two Generations: Grandfather and Grandson: This narrative explores the relationships between people across two generations, highlighting how they maintain connections and understand each other despite the differences in their times.

Past: Grandfather's Era:

In a small village in India, there lived a man named Ram. He was known for his ability to cultivate strong relationships within the community. Ram's method was simple yet profound: personal interaction and community involvement.

Ram started his day by visiting the local tea stall, where he would meet his friends and other villagers. They would discuss various topics, share their experiences, and offer help to those in need. Ram made it a point to visit his friends' homes, attend community gatherings, and participate in local festivals. He believed that face-to-face communication and shared experiences were the keys to building lasting relationships.

One day, a young boy in the village, whose father had passed away, needed guidance on his education. Ram took it upon himself to mentor the boy, helping him with his studies and offering life advice. Over time, the boy grew up to be a successful engineer, always crediting Ram's support as a pivotal factor in his achievements. Ram's relationships were built on trust, empathy, and the genuine time he invested in people.

Present: Grandson's Era:

Decades later, Ram's grandson, Raj, lives in a bustling city and works in the tech industry. While the essence of building relationships remains the same, the methods have evolved with technology and the fast-paced lifestyle.

Raj uses social media platforms to stay connected with friends and family. He regularly updates his status, shares photos, and comments on his friends' posts. While he doesn't meet them as often in person, the digital interactions help maintain the connection.

Raj also participates in online communities and forums related to his interests and profession. He networks with people globally, exchanging ideas and collaborating on projects. When one of his online friends from another city faced a health crisis, Raj organized a crowdfunding campaign, leveraging his social media reach to raise funds and offer support.

Despite the differences in approach, Raj also values personal interaction. He schedules video calls with his grandparents, visits his parents regularly, and makes it a point to meet his close friends for coffee or dinner whenever possible. Raj's relationships are a blend of digital communication and personal interactions.

The Incident: A Shared Value

One day, Raj decided to visit his ancestral village with his grandfather. During their visit, Raj observed how his grandfather's old friends still maintained their relationships through regular visits and community events. He realized the timeless value of personal interaction and the depth it added to relationships.

Inspired, Raj organized a local meet-up for his online community members, bringing together people who had only interacted digitally. The meet-up was a success, with members sharing their experiences and building stronger bonds.

Ram and Raj's experiences highlight the evolution of cultivating relationships. While the methods have changed—from face-to-face interactions in a close-knit community to digital communication across global networks—the core principles remain the same: trust, empathy, and the willingness to invest time and effort. Both generations show that relationships, whether cultivated through tea stall conversations or online forums, are essential for personal growth and support.

Cultivating a Relationship with Your Wife:

Cultivating a relationship with a wife in the real world involves actively investing time and effort into understanding and supporting each other. It includes sharing responsibilities, making joint decisions, and finding ways to grow together despite life's challenges. Communication plays a crucial role in resolving conflicts, expressing feelings, and maintaining a strong emotional connection. Creating meaningful memories, celebrating achievements, and navigating hardships together are key aspects that deepen the bond and contribute to a fulfilling partnership.

In a bustling city, Rohan and Priya navigated the complexities of married life. Rohan, a dedicated professional, often found himself immersed in work, striving to excel in his career. Priya, equally ambitious, balanced her career aspirations with managing their home and supporting Rohan's endeavors.

Over time, Rohan realized the importance of nurturing his relationship with Priya beyond the demands of their daily routines. He started setting aside dedicated time each week for meaningful conversations and shared activities, such as cooking together or taking evening walks. These moments allowed them to reconnect and strengthen their emotional bond.

Rohan also made a conscious effort to express appreciation for Priya's contributions and acknowledge her achievements. He surprised her with small gestures of affection, like leaving notes of encouragement or planning surprise outings to places they cherished.

Through open communication and mutual respect, Rohan and Priya navigated challenges together, whether it was managing finances, supporting each other during stressful times at work, or making decisions that impacted their future.

As their relationship evolved, Rohan realized that prioritizing quality time, communication, and mutual support were essential not only for maintaining a harmonious marriage but also for fostering a deep and lasting connection with his wife, Priya. Their journey together taught them the value of patience, empathy, and the joy of sharing life's moments, both big and small.

This highlights the importance of actively investing in a relationship with one's wife through understanding, communication, and shared experiences, ultimately nurturing a strong and fulfilling partnership.

"*People will forget what you said, people will forget what you did, but people will never forget how you made them feel. -* **Maya Angelou**"

Beyond Blood: The Unbreakable Bond of Siblings

The bond between siblings is one of the most unique and enduring relationships in life. Siblings share experiences that shape their identities and foster deep connections from childhood through adulthood. This bond is built on shared memories, family traditions, and countless moments of joy and challenge.

Siblings often act as confidants, supporters, and lifelong friends. They understand each other's backgrounds and histories in a way that no one else can, providing a sense of continuity and belonging. This relationship can be marked by playful rivalry, mutual respect, and a deep-seated loyalty that persists through the ups and downs of life.

As they grow, siblings learn to navigate their differences, celebrate each other's successes, and offer comfort in times of need. This dynamic teaches valuable life skills such as empathy, patience, and compromise. The sibling bond evolves, but its core remains a source of strength and companionship, illustrating the enduring power of family connections.

Aarav and Anika grew up in a modest home in the heart of a bustling city. From the beginning, their parents instilled in them the importance of family and the strength of their bond. Aarav, the older of the two, always looked out for his little sister, Anika, guiding her through life's early challenges with a protective eye and a gentle heart.

When Aarav was 18, their father was diagnosed with a severe illness. The medical bills piled up, and their family's financial situation became dire. Aarav had just received a scholarship to study engineering at a prestigious university, a dream he had worked tirelessly to achieve. But seeing his family's struggles, he made a heart-wrenching decision: he deferred his admission and took up multiple jobs to support the household and pay for their father's treatments. Anika, just 16 at the time, watched her brother sacrifice his dreams without hesitation, and her admiration for him grew even stronger.

With Aarav's support, their father's condition stabilized, but the family was still in a fragile state. Anika excelled in school, inspired by her brother's selflessness, and won a scholarship to study medicine abroad. She hesitated to leave Aarav, knowing how much he had given up for the family. But Aarav, ever the supportive brother, encouraged her to pursue her dreams. "You have to go," he told her. "This is your chance to make a difference, to achieve what you've always wanted."

While Anika was away, she studied diligently and sent home as much money as she could from her part-time jobs. Aarav continued to work hard, taking evening classes to eventually finish his engineering degree. Despite the distance, their bond remained unbroken. They spoke every day, sharing their struggles and successes, each conversation a reminder of their unwavering support for each other.

Years later, Anika returned home as a qualified doctor. Her first job was at a local hospital, and her salary provided much-needed stability for the family. With Anika's help, Aarav finally pursued his passion fully, landing a job at a renowned engineering firm. Their sacrifices had paid off, and they had built a life where both could thrive.

However, life had one more test in store for them. Anika was diagnosed with a rare illness that required specialized treatment abroad. The costs were astronomical, and once again, Aarav faced a choice. Without hesitation, he sold his house and liquidated his savings to fund Anika's treatment. "You've got to get better," he told her. "You're the light of our family."

Anika, touched by her brother's unwavering devotion, fought through her illness with all her strength. Her recovery was slow but steady, and she emerged stronger, driven by the love and sacrifices of her brother. Once healthy, she vowed to give back to Aarav the opportunities he had given her.

With her connections in the medical field, Anika helped Aarav secure funding to start his engineering firm, fulfilling his long-held dream. Together, they turned the firm into a successful enterprise, giving back to the community that had supported them during their hardest times.

Through every trial and triumph, Aarav and Anika's bond only deepened. Their story became a testament to the power of sibling love and sacrifice. They proved that family is not just about blood but about the unwavering support, sacrifices, and unbreakable bond that withstands the test of time.

"From birth to the end of our lives, we form countless relationships, each unique in its way. These range from the bonds with our parents and siblings to those with friends, spouses, and children. While all these relationships are deeply cherished, they often contain elements of incompleteness or hidden truths. However, one relationship stands out as an exception—the bond between siblings.

Siblings know everything about each other, from favorite foods to personal preferences, and all the good and bad traits. Despite this deep understanding, they often engage in playful teasing. This behavior is not born out of animosity but rather as a way to keep life interesting. Constantly displaying affection can become monotonous, and unlike the pretenses of affection shown elsewhere, siblings find no need to feign love at home.

Their playful bickering is unique to their relationship because they understand it will never be taken to heart. They will always support each other, whether it's helping with studies, securing a job, or providing financial stability. Siblings quarrel only with each other, confident in the knowledge that they will always have each other's backs, no matter what.

Always remember, if you ever find yourself in a difficult situation or need to share something personal, your sibling should be the first person you turn to. Cultivate a bond where your sibling is your foremost confidant. There is nothing more significant than the sibling relationship because you share common parents who always have your best interests at heart. They provide the most genuine love and guidance.

If your family is facing any issues that are causing significant distress to your parents, sit down and discuss it with your siblings. You'll be surprised at how this can lead to resolving the problem. Even if the issue remains unresolved, it will undoubtedly alleviate some of the stress your parents are experiencing."

5
Nurturing Love

Love is a powerful force that transcends boundaries. We explore the intricacies of romantic love, self-love, and platonic love, emphasizing the importance of nurturing genuine connections that enrich our lives.

Nurturing love involves actively fostering and maintaining a deep and meaningful connection with another person. It requires consistent effort, understanding, and communication.

Love is more than just an emotion; it is a deliberate choice to care for, support, and grow with another person. In a world that often moves at a relentless pace, nurturing love requires intentional effort and dedication. This book explores the multifaceted journey of nurturing love, offering insights and practical advice on how to build and sustain deep, meaningful relationships.

- **The Foundation of Trust and Honesty:** Every strong relationship is built on trust and honesty. It's essential to cultivate a foundation of transparency and reliability, creating a safe space where love can flourish. By consistently being truthful and dependable, you nurture a bond that can withstand any challenge.
- **The Power of Empathy and Support:** Understanding and sharing the feelings of your partner is crucial in nurturing love. Providing unwavering support through life's challenges and joys strengthens your emotional connection. By actively listening and showing empathy, you demonstrate that you value and care for your partner's experiences and emotions.
- **Quality Time:** Spending quality time together is vital for any relationship. From engaging in shared activities to enjoying simple

moments of togetherness, these experiences create lasting memories and deepen your bond. Prioritizing time for each other helps maintain a strong connection amid busy schedules.

- **Respect and Appreciation:** Respecting each other's individuality and expressing appreciation for the little things are fundamental for a healthy relationship. Maintaining mutual respect and showing gratitude fosters a positive and supportive environment. Recognizing and valuing each other's contributions strengthens your partnership.
- **Patience and Understanding:** No relationship is without its challenges. Patience and understanding are key to navigating conflicts and growing stronger together. By approaching disagreements with a calm and open mind, you can turn potential obstacles into opportunities for deeper connection and mutual growth.
- **The Art of Communication:** Effective communication is the lifeblood of any relationship. Improving your communication skills ensures that both partners feel heard and valued. Techniques such as active listening, clear expression of thoughts and feelings, and constructive feedback help maintain a healthy dialogue.
- **Shared Goals and Growth:** Setting shared goals and growing together as individuals can enhance your relationship. Supporting each other's dreams and aspirations fosters a sense of teamwork and shared purpose. By encouraging personal growth and celebrating each other's achievements, you build a stronger, more united partnership.
- **Maintaining the Spark:** Over time, keeping the romance alive can be challenging. Creative ways to maintain the spark include planning special dates, surprising each other with thoughtful gestures, and continually finding joy and excitement in your relationship. Keeping the romance fresh helps sustain a loving connection.
- **Love in the Digital Age:** Navigating the complexities of nurturing love in a technologically-driven world is crucial. Balancing digital communication with meaningful, in-person interactions ensures that your relationship remains personal and intimate. Understanding how to effectively integrate technology into your relationship can enhance, rather than hinder, your connection.

Nurturing love is a lifelong journey that requires commitment, effort, and a willingness to grow together. It reflects the continuous process of building and sustaining a loving, resilient relationship.

"*Love can happen with anyone—it could be with pets, animals, minors, elderly people, classmates, colleagues, relatives, neighbors, and others. Therefore, don't feel hesitant to express your affection. It should always be grounded in mutual understanding, ensuring that no one experiences any harm or loss.*"

Historical Perspectives on Love:

Explore how the concept of love has evolved. Delve into different cultural and historical contexts to understand how love and relationships were nurtured in ancient civilizations, through the Middle Ages, and into modern times.

1. Love in Ancient Times:

In ancient times, love was often intertwined with cultural, social, and economic factors that significantly influenced how relationships were formed and nurtured.

- **Ancient Egypt:** Love and partnership were highly valued. The famous love story of Cleopatra and Mark Antony can illustrate the passionate and strategic aspects of relationships during that era.
- **Ancient India:** Romantic love in ancient India was deeply embedded in myths and literature, often highlighting themes of devotion and sacrifice. Stories like that of Shakuntala and Dushyanta, from the Mahabharata and Kalidasa's play, illustrate the profound connection and enduring love between the protagonists. These tales celebrate the emotional depth and spiritual aspects of love, showcasing its power to transcend challenges and societal norms.

2. Medieval and Renaissance Love:

Medieval and Renaissance Love encompasses the romantic and philosophical ideas about love that developed during the Medieval and Renaissance periods in Europe. These concepts significantly influenced how love and relationships were perceived and expressed in Western culture.

- **Courtly Love:** During the Middle Ages, courtly love was a chivalric romance emphasizing nobility and idealized love. The tales of Lancelot and Guinevere can serve as examples.
- **Shakespearean Love:** William Shakespeare's works, like "Romeo and Juliet," reflect the intensity and tragedy of young love, providing timeless insights into human emotions.

Real-Life Examples:

There are many different real-life stories of couples who exemplify the principles of nurturing love. These public figures are those whose experiences offer valuable lessons.

1. Historical Figures:

We explore how historical figures have embodied and influenced the ideals of love, marriage, and relationships. Their lives and legacies provide valuable lessons and inspiration for fostering loving and enduring partnerships.

- **Pierre and Marie Curie:** Their partnership in life and science illustrates how mutual respect, shared goals, and collaboration can nurture love and lead to extraordinary achievements.
- **Franklin and Eleanor Roosevelt:** Their relationship shows how couples can support each other through personal and political challenges, demonstrating resilience and partnership.

2. Modern Examples:

We explore how modern figures have embodied and influenced the ideals of love, marriage, and relationships. Their lives and legacies provide valuable lessons and inspiration for fostering loving and enduring partnerships.

- **Barack and Michelle Obama:** Their relationship provides insights into balancing demanding careers while maintaining a strong family bond and mutual support.

- **Everyday Couples**: Include anecdotes from couples of different backgrounds and cultures who have successfully nurtured their love over decades. These stories can highlight diverse strategies and universal truths about sustaining relationships.

Inspirational Stories:

These stories can highlight the impact of love on personal growth and resilience.

- **Helen Keller and Anne Sullivan:** Though not a romantic relationship, their bond showcases how love and dedication can overcome significant obstacles, providing a powerful example of nurturing a supportive and transformative connection.
- **War-time Love Letters:** Include excerpts from letters written by soldiers and their loved ones during wars. These heartfelt communications show how love can endure and strengthen despite physical separation and hardships.

Conflict Resolution:

Conflict Resolution in nurturing love involves effectively managing and resolving disagreements or disputes that arise in a relationship.

- **Scenario-Based Advice:** Take guidance on common relationship challenges by presenting practical solutions. For instance, addressing financial stress, balancing work and personal life, or navigating family dynamics.
- **Communication Exercises:** Couples can engage in activities such as active listening sessions, open-ended question games, and regular check-ins to enhance their communication and understanding.

Building Traditions:

Building Traditions in nurturing love refers to the process of creating new, meaningful practices and rituals within a relationship that help strengthen the bond between partners. These traditions can be small, everyday habits or special rituals reserved for significant occasions.

- **Creating Rituals:** Share ideas for creating meaningful traditions and rituals that can help couples stay connected. This could include regular date nights, anniversary celebrations, or simple daily habits that reinforce their bond.

Emphasize the importance of continuous effort, adaptability, and the joy that comes from nurturing a loving relationship.

The Price of Image:

In a bustling city in India, Priya and Raj fell deeply in love during their college years. They were inseparable, dreaming of a future together. However, their happiness was short-lived. Priya's parents, deeply entrenched in traditional values and concerned about their societal image, disapproved of Raj. They believed that his lower social standing would tarnish their family's reputation.

Despite Priya's heartfelt pleas, her parents arranged her marriage to a wealthy businessman. The wedding was grand, and celebrated by society as a perfect match, but Priya was heartbroken. She moved to her new home, where she felt trapped and alone. Her husband was indifferent, and the house, though lavish, felt cold and empty.

Back home, Priya's family faced a series of misfortunes. Her father fell ill, and her younger brother met with an accident. Her mother, overwhelmed by the stress, suffered a stroke. Within a few years, the once vibrant household was struck by a wave of grief and loss.

Priya's guardians, now looking back, regretted their decision. They realized that their choice, driven by societal pressures, had brought misery not just to Priya but to the entire family. They had focused on maintaining their image rather than prioritizing their daughter's happiness.

This story underscores a powerful lesson: when people are alive, decisions should be made to foster happiness. Decisions driven by societal expectations often lead to sorrow. It is essential to prioritize the well-being and happiness of those involved. True contentment comes from choosing paths where everyone can be happy, rather than conforming to external pressures.

Love Knows No Boundaries:

Love can happen anywhere and with anyone; it doesn't have to be with someone of a different gender. Same-gender attraction is also real, and the important thing is that partners should be happy together. Some people say that same-gender attraction is impossible and just a state of mind, even calling it an illness that should be avoided. However, they don't understand how same-gender couples feel inside. They experience the same emotions as anyone else would if told to stay away from their loved ones. Every love story has the same feelings, so no one should judge. Everyone has the right to choose their partner, whether a boy or a girl or a transgender.

> "*As you all might have seen in web series or movies these days, there is a lot of emphasis on same-sex marriage and gay or lesbian relationships. Some people argue that this is just a baseless trend and consider it an illness, but that is not the case. It's possible that such relationships existed in the past, but people didn't have the courage to speak about them. Now, individuals have gained the power to accept themselves, and movies and shows are made to convey that these relationships are normal. We should not label them as illnesses but instead accept them as normal because it doesn't affect us directly. We don't know how they feel when we embarrass them, so we should be kind to all relationships.*"

Choices for True Happiness:

Two young women, Aisha and Meera, lived in a small, picturesque town nestled between rolling hills and lush forests. Their friendship had blossomed from childhood, a bond so deep that they often felt they could communicate without words. As they grew older, their connection evolved into something more profound, something that neither of them had anticipated.

Aisha and Meera's story was one of quiet, tender moments and unspoken understanding. They shared dreams and fears, laughter and tears. Over time, their feelings for each other grew, transcending the boundaries of mere friendship.

It was a love that defied the traditional expectations of their community, a love that was both beautiful and challenging.

In a society where same-gender love was often misunderstood and unaccepted, Aisha and Meera found strength in each other. They navigated their relationship with care and courage, knowing that their journey would not be easy. Yet, they remained steadfast, drawing inspiration from the love stories that came before them and those that would follow.

Their story is a testament to the fact that love knows no boundaries, no rules, and no limitations. It is a reminder that everyone has their own story, unique and precious and that every story deserves to be told.

The Importance of Caring for Parents:

In today's fast-paced world, it's common for children to move away from their parents in pursuit of education, career opportunities, or personal growth. However, it's crucial to remember the importance of caring for our parents, especially as they age and become more vulnerable.

Parents spend their lives nurturing and supporting their children, often sacrificing their dreams and desires. As children grow up and start their own lives, parents may find themselves feeling lonely and neglected. The house that was once filled with laughter and activity becomes quiet and empty. This transition can be particularly hard on parents who may already be facing health issues or other challenges associated with aging.

In many cases, children move to different cities or even countries for better job prospects. While the financial rewards may be higher, the emotional cost can be significant. Is earning more money truly worth it if it means leaving your parents to face their struggles alone? It's essential to consider whether the additional income compensates for the guilt and sorrow of knowing your parents are suffering in your absence.

For some, the solution might be to find a job closer to home, even if it means earning a bit less. This way, you can be there to provide emotional and physical support to your parents. If daily commuting isn't possible, at least try to visit them on weekends or as frequently as your schedule allows. Regular visits can make a world of difference, providing your parents with the companionship and reassurance they need.

Sometimes, parents themselves may encourage their children to move away, prioritizing their children's career growth and future over their comfort. While their intentions are noble, it's important to balance career aspirations with familial responsibilities. The extent to which you consider and care for your parents is a reflection of your values and priorities.

If you choose a job close to home or work from home because your parents, neighbors, and relatives might taunt you, asking why you don't switch to a better company. You need to just smile and brush it off without explaining to everyone why you work close to home. If you try to justify yourself to everyone, you will eventually become frustrated and consider moving away. Moving away isn't wrong if your siblings or someone else is already there to take care of your parents.

Ultimately, maintaining a connection with your parents isn't just about fulfilling an obligation; it's about honoring the love and sacrifices they've made for you. By ensuring their well-being and happiness, you not only repay their kindness but also create a stronger, more meaningful bond that enriches both of your lives. After all, the essence of family lies in being there for each other through thick and thin, regardless of the physical distance that may separate you.

"Your task is not to seek for love, but merely to seek and find all the barriers within yourself that you have built against it. - **Rumi***"*

6
Re-Defining Marriage

Marriage is a cornerstone of society, but it's time to redefine its meaning. We discuss modern approaches to partnership, consent, and equality, shedding light on how to build fulfilling relationships on your terms.

The phrase "re-defining marriage" is often used in discussions and debates surrounding changes to the legal definition or societal understanding of marriage. Historically, marriage has been defined in various ways across different cultures and societies, often centered around the union between a man and a woman. However, in recent decades, there have been significant shifts in how marriage is understood and legally recognized in many parts of the world.

The concept of "re-defining marriage" typically refers to efforts to broaden the legal definition of marriage to include unions beyond those between a man and a woman. This can include the recognition of same-sex marriages, polygamous marriages, or other forms of consensual adult partnerships.

Advocates for redefining marriage argue that marriage should be a fundamental human right accessible to all individuals regardless of sexual orientation or gender identity. They often emphasize principles of equality, fairness, and the importance of recognizing and protecting the relationships and families of LGBTQ+ individuals.

"LGBT is an initialism that stands for "lesbian, gay, bisexual, and transgender". It may refer to anyone who is non-heterosexual, non-heteroromantic, or non-cisgender, instead of exclusively to people who are lesbian, gay, bisexual, or transgender."

Opponents of redefining marriage may argue from religious, cultural, or traditional perspectives, asserting that marriage has a specific historical and social purpose that should be preserved. They may express concerns about the potential consequences of altering the traditional definition of marriage, including impacts on family structures, religious freedom, and societal values.

The debate over redefining marriage has been particularly prominent in discussions surrounding the legalization of same-sex marriage in various countries. This issue has sparked significant legal battles, social movements, and political controversies around the world. Ultimately, decisions about whether or how to redefine marriage are often shaped by complex interactions between legal, cultural, religious, and political factors within each society.

The Evolution of Marriage Should Be:

Here, we will learn about the evolution of marriage through a few key points

1. **Historical Context:** Marriage has a rich historical background where its primary purpose varied from culture to culture. Traditionally, marriages were often arranged by families to forge alliances, secure economic stability, or preserve social status. In many societies, love was not the central focus of marriage. Over time, especially in Western societies, the notion of marriage evolved to prioritize romantic love and personal compatibility. This shift reflects broader societal changes, including the emphasis on individualism and personal happiness. Examining these historical shifts can provide a deeper understanding of how current definitions of marriage came to be.

2. **Legal Changes:** Legal changes have played a crucial role in redefining marriage. For example, the introduction of the "Special Marriage Act" in India allows for civil marriages irrespective of religion, breaking the constraints of traditional matrimonial customs. Similarly, the legalization of same-sex marriage in countries like the United States, Canada, and many European nations represents a significant redefinition. These legal reforms often follow prolonged social and political struggles and reflect changing societal values towards equality and individual rights.

3. **Cultural Shifts:** Cultural shifts also contribute to the redefinition of marriage. In urban areas, the concept of marriage may be more liberal, with greater acceptance of love marriages, inter-caste or interfaith marriages, and even live-in relationships. In contrast, rural areas might hold more traditional views. These cultural shifts are influenced by education, exposure to different lifestyles through media and travel, and economic independence, especially among women. Exploring these variations provides insight into how marriage should be perceived and practiced differently within the same country.

4. **Technological Impact:** Technology has revolutionized how people meet and form relationships, significantly impacting marriage. Online dating platforms and matrimonial websites have made it easier for people to find partners who match their preferences. Long-distance relationships are more manageable with communication technologies like video calls and instant messaging. Furthermore, social media plays a role in how relationships are perceived and maintained. Technology also raises questions about privacy, authenticity, and the quality of relationships formed online, all of which contribute to the evolving concept of marriage.

5. **Economic Factors:** The economic landscape has a profound influence on marriage. The increasing participation of women in the workforce has led to a shift in traditional gender roles within marriage. Dual-income households are more common, and financial independence allows individuals, especially women, to make marriage choices based on personal preference rather than economic necessity. Economic stability is also a significant factor in the decision to marry, delay marriage, or forgo it altogether. Additionally, economic disparities and job instability can impact marital satisfaction and stability.

6. **Social Acceptance:** The growing acceptance of LGBTQ+ marriages is a critical aspect of redefining marriage. Societal attitudes towards same-sex relationships have become more accepting in many parts of the world, leading to legal recognition and equal rights. This shift is supported by inclusive policies, education, and awareness campaigns. The recognition of LGBTQ+ marriages challenges traditional definitions and promotes a more inclusive understanding of love and partnership. This acceptance also extends to other non-traditional relationships, such as those involving transgender or non-binary individuals.

7. **Ethical and Moral Perspectives:** Redefining marriage brings ethical and moral questions to the forefront. Issues such as surrogacy and adoption raise questions about the rights of children, the responsibilities of parents, and the implications for family dynamics. For example, commercial surrogacy involves ethical debates about exploitation and the rights of surrogate mothers. Adoption by same-sex couples or single parents can also raise moral questions in different cultural and religious contexts.

8. **Global Perspectives:** Different countries and cultures have unique approaches to redefining marriage. For instance, Scandinavian countries are known for their progressive marriage laws, including recognizing civil unions and same-sex marriages early on. In contrast, some Middle Eastern and African countries maintain more traditional views and strict marriage laws. These global perspectives are shaped by cultural, religious, and legal factors. Understanding these differences highlights the diversity in how marriage is perceived and practiced worldwide, reflecting broader social, political, and cultural contexts.

9. **Personal Narratives:** Sharing personal narratives of individuals who have experienced redefining marriage can provide valuable insights. These stories might include accounts from same-sex couples who fought for legal recognition, individuals in open or polyamorous relationships, or those who chose to remain childless by choice. Personal narratives highlight the human aspect of these changes, illustrating the challenges, triumphs, and everyday realities of living in a marriage that defies traditional norms.

10. **Future Predictions:** Speculating on the future of marriage involves considering current trends and emerging technologies. For example, the increasing use of artificial intelligence and robotics in daily life raises questions about human-robot relationships and their potential recognition. Societal expectations are also shifting, with younger generations often prioritizing personal growth and career over traditional marriage. Future predictions might include greater acceptance of diverse family structures, changes in legal frameworks to accommodate new forms of relationships, and evolving cultural norms around partnership and commitment.

These detailed explanations provide a comprehensive view of how the concept of marriage is being redefined across various dimensions.

Examples of Re-Defining Marriage:

It illustrates various ways in which the concept of marriage has been expanded or altered:

- **Same-Sex Marriage:** One of the most prominent examples is the legalization of same-sex marriage. This redefinition includes marriages between two people of the same gender, challenging the traditional notion of marriage as exclusively between a man and a woman. Countries like the Netherlands, Canada, and the United States have legalized same-sex marriage, recognizing it as equal to heterosexual marriage.
- **Polygamous and Polyamorous Relationships:** In some cultures and societies, marriage is being redefined to include multiple spouses. Polygamy, where one individual has multiple spouses, has been traditionally practiced in various cultures and religions. In more modern contexts, polyamorous relationships, where people engage in consensual relationships with multiple partners, are also gaining recognition, although not always with legal marriage rights.
- **Interfaith and Intercultural Marriages:** Marriages between individuals of different faiths or cultural backgrounds are increasingly common. These marriages often require a redefinition of traditional practices and beliefs to accommodate and respect both partners' backgrounds.
- **Gender-Neutral and Non-Binary Recognition:** Some regions are redefining marriage to be more inclusive of gender diversity. This includes recognizing and allowing marriages for individuals who identify as non-binary, genderqueer, or transgender, ensuring that marriage laws are not limited by traditional gender binaries.
- **Childless Marriages by Choice:** Traditionally, marriage has often been linked to procreation. However, many modern couples are choosing to remain childless by choice. This redefinition of marriage emphasizes the companionship, partnership, and mutual support aspects of marriage, rather than its role in family expansion.
- **Open Marriages:** Some couples are redefining marriage by choosing to have open marriages, where both partners agree to engage in sexual or romantic relationships with other people. This challenges the traditional notion of marital fidelity and monogamy.

- **Long-Distance Marriages:** With globalization and increased mobility, some marriages are redefined by geography. Couples may live in different cities or countries due to work or personal preferences, maintaining their marriage through digital communication and periodic visits.
- **Marriage as Partnership of Equals:** Historically, many marriages were based on clearly defined gender roles, often with a dominant/submissive dynamic. Modern marriages are increasingly based on equality, with both partners sharing responsibilities and decision-making equally, regardless of gender.
- **Non-Legalized Commitment Ceremonies:** Some couples choose to have commitment ceremonies without legal marriage. These ceremonies can carry the same personal and social significance as a legal marriage but without legal recognition and obligations.

These examples show how the concept of marriage is evolving to become more inclusive and reflective of diverse human relationships and identities.

Love Across Boundaries and Standing Against Dowry: The Perfect Marriage

There was a boy named Vicky and a girl named Priya who loved each other deeply. They decided it was time to inform their families and involve them in their relationship. When they broke the news to their families, Vicky's family opposed the match because Vicky and Priya belonged to different castes. Vicky tried to convince his parents by explaining that he had known Priya for five years and that she was a wonderful person who would love and respect everyone in the family. He emphasized that she could manage both her career and their household.

After some struggle, Vicky's parents finally agreed to the marriage. The families set a date for the wedding, and as it approached, Vicky's father brought up the topic of dowry. He mentioned to Vicky that although they understood dowry was wrong, they were concerned about societal perceptions. They worried people would think it strange that their well-educated son was getting married without receiving any dowry, including a car or money.

Vicky responded firmly, "Dad, I am strongly against dowry. I can manage all our expenses myself. What's the point of my education if I have to depend on Priya's family for a car or something else? I can't accept dowry, even if they offer it. If it comes to that, I would rather not go through with the marriage than accept dowry."

His parents, though initially resistant, started to appreciate his perspective. Despite their societal concerns, they respected Vicky's stand and decided to support him in rejecting dowry.

New Beginnings and Respect for Space:

Vicky and Priya got married, and then Vicky's parents suggested that the couple live near their workplace to give them some personal space. Vicky initially refused, saying they didn't need it, but his parents insisted. Deep down, they worried that since it was a love marriage, Priya might struggle to adjust, potentially leading to daily arguments.

Vicky and Priya moved into their new place together. After a month, Priya expressed her desire for Vicky's parents to live with them. Overjoyed, Vicky called his parents and invited them to come stay with them. His parents were happy to join them in their home.

Embracing Family and Defying Traditions:

Vicky's parents came to visit them. However, they declined to stay with them permanently, although they were secretly very happy. Priya explained to them, "You are not just like my parents; you are my parents because you accepted me despite being from a different caste and agreed to a dowry-free marriage. Only true parents could do that. How can I leave you alone at this age, especially when you didn't demand anything from my parents? I genuinely mean it when I say I respect and consider you as my own. Please stay with us."

Moved by Priya's words, Vicky's parents felt proud of their son and daughter-in-law and agreed to stay with them. Priya adjusted their belongings in the house and even arranged their clothes in her wardrobe. When her mother-in-law suggested that Priya should keep her room separate, Priya replied, "If I were your daughter, we wouldn't have separate wardrobes. We should live the same way now as we did before the wedding. People have changed a lot in the name of privacy, but privacy doesn't mean having separate rooms."

The whole family started living happily together. Months and years passed smoothly. There were occasional misunderstandings and clashes due to different perspectives, but Priya was very understanding. If she ever said something hurtful, she would later explain to her mother-in-law that sometimes words can hurt, but that shouldn't weaken their relationship. She would say, "I can get upset with you just like Vicky does sometimes, and you can get upset with me, but we are family, and we will always stay together."

Seeing Priya's behavior, Vicky's parents realized they had never been as happy, even with their caste and dowry. Over time, Vicky bought a car, and the whole family lived a happy and fulfilling life together.

From the story above, I don't mean to suggest that marriages within the same caste are not good. My point is simply to show that people can be happy even if they marry someone from a different caste.

Thriving Together: Keys to a Happy Married Life:

It will focus on several modern and progressive concepts that challenge traditional norms and emphasize equality, mutual respect, and personal fulfillment.

- **Mutual Respect and Understanding:** Both partners should respect each other's individuality, opinions, and needs. Understanding each other's perspectives and communicating openly can help resolve conflicts and build a stronger bond.
- **Effective Communication:** Open and honest communication is crucial. Discussing daily activities, sharing feelings, and talking through issues can prevent misunderstandings and foster a healthy relationship.
- **Equality and Partnership:** Marriage should be a partnership where both partners share responsibilities, whether it's household chores, financial management, or decision-making. Equality in the relationship can lead to a more harmonious and balanced life together.
- **Support and Encouragement:** Supporting each other's dreams, ambitions, and personal growth is important. Encouraging each other through challenges and celebrating successes together can strengthen the marital bond.
- **Quality Time Together:** Spending quality time together, engaging in shared activities, and making efforts to keep the romance alive can help maintain a strong emotional connection.
- **Trust and Loyalty:** Trust is the foundation of any strong relationship. Being honest, reliable, and loyal to each other fosters a sense of security and deepens the relationship.
- **Conflict Resolution:** Every relationship faces conflicts. Handling disagreements with patience, listening to each other, and finding compromises can help in resolving issues without causing lasting damage to the relationship.
- **Balance of Personal Space and Togetherness:** While spending time together is important, giving each other personal space and time for

individual interests and hobbies is also crucial. This balance helps maintain individuality within the relationship.

- **Adaptability and Growth:** Being open to change and willing to grow together as individuals and as a couple can help in navigating the different phases of married life.
- **Family and Social Relationships:** Maintaining healthy relationships with each other's families and friends can provide additional support and enrich the couple's social life.

> "*In a marriage, both the husband and wife should equally care for each other's families. Since the wife leaves her own home to join her husband's family, special attention should be given to her needs and comfort. This mutual care and respect for each other's families help in building a strong, supportive, and harmonious relationship.*"

Marry the Right Person, Not the Age:

Absolutely! Marriage should be decided upon when you find the right person you truly like, rather than just because you've reached the so-called "marriageable age." Marriage is a relationship built on love, respect, and understanding, and these qualities are far more important than age.

It's better to marry when you find the right partner because that's when both of you can create a beautiful life together. When two people marry out of mutual choice and affection, they appreciate and understand each other's needs and significance, which strengthens and enriches the relationship.

It's essential to realize that the purpose of marriage should not be to merely fulfill societal expectations but to bring someone into your life who stands by you through every joy and sorrow.

> "*Marriage is not about age; it's about finding the right person. -* **Sophia Bush**"

Freedom For Tomorrow: Ending Child Marriage:

Re-defining marriage to stop child marriage involves advocating for policies and societal norms that prioritize the protection and rights of children. It aims to eradicate the harmful practice of marrying children off at a young age, which deprives them of their childhood, education, and future opportunities. By promoting laws that set a minimum age for marriage, providing access to education for all children, and raising awareness about the consequences of child marriage, societies can ensure that every child has the chance to grow up in a safe and nurturing environment, free from the burden of premature marital responsibilities.

In a rural village nestled among lush green fields, young Ayesha lived with her parents and younger siblings. A bright-eyed girl with dreams of becoming a teacher, Ayesha loved spending her days at school, where she excelled in her studies and cherished time with friends.

One summer afternoon, everything changed. Ayesha's parents, struggling with financial hardships, received a proposal from a wealthy family in a neighboring village for Ayesha to marry their son, a man twice her age. Shocked and fearful, Ayesha's dreams of finishing school and pursuing her passion for teaching were shattered.

Terrified at the thought of leaving her education behind and marrying a stranger, Ayesha confided in her school teacher, Mr. Sharma. Moved by Ayesha's plight, Mr. Sharma sprang into action. He approached community leaders, organized meetings with local parents, and started an awareness campaign about the harms of child marriage.

Through tireless advocacy and collaboration with like-minded individuals, Mr. Sharma managed to persuade Ayesha's parents and the prospective groom's family to reconsider their decision. With support from the village elders and authorities, they intervened to prevent the marriage and instead ensured Ayesha's continued education.

Empowered by her community's support, Ayesha returned to school with renewed determination. She became a vocal advocate against child marriage, sharing her story to inspire other girls and families to prioritize education and delay marriage until adulthood.

Ayesha's courage and the community's proactive measures not only saved her from an early marriage but also sparked a movement in the village to protect children's rights and promote their education. Together, they laid the foundation for a future where every child could dream freely and pursue their ambitions without the threat of premature marriage.

If child marriage were to occur, the circumstances would typically involve:

- **Loss of Education:** The child, usually a girl, is forced to drop out of school, depriving her of educational opportunities crucial for personal development and future independence.
- **Health Risks:** Early pregnancy poses significant health risks to the young bride, including complications during childbirth, maternal mortality, and issues related to physical and psychological immaturity.
- **Social Isolation:** The child bride often faces social isolation from peers and limited opportunities for social interaction, inhibiting personal growth and integration into broader society.
- **Economic Dependence:** With limited education and skills, the child bride becomes economically dependent on her spouse and his family, perpetuating cycles of poverty and vulnerability.
- **Psychological Impact:** The emotional and psychological toll of being married off at a young age can lead to mental health issues, such as depression and anxiety, stemming from a lack of autonomy and unmet developmental needs.
- **Legal Vulnerability:** Child brides are often unable to advocate for their rights or access legal protections, leaving them vulnerable to abuse, exploitation, and marital violence.

These circumstances underscore the urgent need to prevent child marriage through legislative measures, community education, and support systems that prioritize children's rights, safety, and well-being.

Evaluating Marriage Prospects: Beyond Financial Considerations

In many cultures, financial status often plays a significant role in marriage decisions. Families may prioritize wealth and financial stability when considering potential suitors, aiming for alliances that promise economic advantages. This focus on financial resources can overshadow other crucial qualities, such as personal character, mutual compatibility, and shared values.

However, it's essential to recognize that a successful marriage is not solely dependent on financial wealth. An average individual, with their own set of virtues and strengths, can also offer a loving and supportive partnership. True compatibility, understanding, and emotional connection often outweigh monetary considerations, contributing to a more fulfilling and enduring relationship.

Evaluating marriage prospects should involve a holistic view that considers not only financial aspects but also the potential for a strong, supportive, and genuine partnership.

Beyond Wealth: A Story of True Compatibility

In a vibrant city, lived Ananya, a bright and ambitious young woman with a passion for education. Her family was affluent, and many expected her to marry well, with financial stability often seen as a primary criterion. When Ananya was introduced to Aryan, the son of a wealthy businessman, there was initial excitement. Aryan was charming and well-off, and many saw him as an ideal match for Ananya.

As the courtship progressed, Aryan's financial success and social status made him a highly desirable candidate. However, despite his many admirable qualities, Ananya couldn't help but feel that something was missing. Their conversations rarely delved into her interests or aspirations; instead, they focused on social events and material possessions.

Meanwhile, Ananya had also met Rohan, a humble but exceptionally driven educator. Rohan's background was modest, but his passion for teaching and his dedication to making a difference in the community deeply resonated with her. He valued education and personal growth, and their conversations were filled with intellectual discussions and mutual respect.

As Ananya's engagement to Aryan progressed, she found herself increasingly conflicted. While Aryan offered financial security, she felt a deeper connection with Rohan. She realized that true partnership meant more than financial stability; it required emotional support, shared values, and a genuine understanding of one another's goals.

In a courageous decision, Ananya chose to end her engagement with Aryan. She faced societal pressures and disappointed expectations, but her heart was set on a different path. She chose to marry Rohan, who not only appreciated her ambitions but also shared her values and dreams.

Their marriage was a testament to the power of choosing a partner based on genuine compatibility rather than financial advantages. Despite their modest means, Ananya and Rohan built a life filled with mutual respect, intellectual stimulation, and unwavering support. They supported each other's dreams and created a nurturing environment for personal and professional growth.

In the end, Ananya's decision proved that true fulfillment in a relationship comes from understanding, shared values, and emotional connection. Her story highlighted that sometimes, choosing a partner with a modest financial background but rich in qualities like passion and dedication can lead to a more profound and satisfying partnership.

In conclusion, I would like to emphasize that none of these external factors matter – it doesn't matter whom you marry, what their caste is, what their skin color is, or how much either of them earns. What truly matters is the understanding they share, the feelings they have for each other, and the happiness they bring into each other's lives.

*"A successful marriage requires falling in love many times, always with the same person. - **Mignon McLaughlin**"*

7

Dowry: Breaking the Chains

Dowry has long been a symbol of inequality and oppression. We confront this outdated practice, advocating for its abolition and championing a future where marriage is based on love and respect, not financial transactions.

Dowry, traditionally practiced in many cultures, involves the transfer of substantial gifts or money from the bride's family to the groom's family upon marriage. While deeply rooted in tradition, this practice often perpetuates financial strain, gender inequality, and social injustice. Rejecting dowry represents a significant shift towards promoting equality and justice within society.

Historical Origins and Evolution of the Dowry System:

It refers to the examination of the beginnings and development of the practice of providing a dowry, tracing its roots in ancient customs and societies, and understanding how it has changed and adapted over time across different cultures and regions.

Ancient Practices:

Ancient Practices in the context of dowry refer to the traditional customs and rituals associated with the transfer of wealth, property, or gifts from the bride's family to the groom or his family upon marriage. These practices have deep historical roots and vary widely across different cultures and regions.

- **Dowry as a Pre-Inheritance:** In ancient times, dowry was often seen as a way for parents to give their daughters a share of the family wealth before their inheritance. It was a form of financial security for the bride.
- **Bride Price:** In some cultures, the groom's family paid a price to the bride's family, which could be seen as a precursor to or variation of the dowry system.

Medieval Period:

The Medieval Period, spanning roughly from the 5th to the late 15th century, saw the development and institutionalization of many social practices, including the dowry system.

- **Property and Status:** During the medieval period, dowries were used to forge alliances between powerful families. The amount and quality of dowry often reflected the bride's family's social status.
- **Economic Transactions:** Dowries were also economic transactions that helped to maintain the wealth and status of families. They were used to buy land, pay off debts, or establish businesses.

Colonial Era:

The Colonial Era, particularly during the British rule in India (approximately from the mid-18th century to the mid-20th century), had a significant impact on various social practices, including the dowry system.

- **Codification of Dowry:** In some regions, the colonial powers codified dowry practices into law, which sometimes reinforced the system. For example, British colonial laws in India formalized dowry as a legal practice.
- **Shift in Perception:** Over time, dowry became more about the financial obligations of the bride's family rather than the bride's security.

Evolution Over Time:

Evolution Over Time in the context of dowry refers to how the practice and perception of dowry have changed across different periods in history or within a particular cultural context. This evolution can include shifts in the reasons for giving dowry, changes in the items or wealth exchanged, alterations in societal attitudes towards dowry, legal reforms, and how modernization and education have impacted the practice.

- **Transition from Voluntary to Compulsory:** Initially, dowries were voluntary gifts from the bride's family. Over time, they became compulsory and often exorbitant demands by the groom's family.
- **Economic and Social Pressures:** With increasing economic pressures, dowries have become a significant financial burden on the bride's family. This has led to dowry-related debts, poverty, and even dowry deaths.
- **Legal Reforms and Resistance:** Various countries have implemented legal reforms to combat the dowry system. For instance, the Dowry Prohibition Act in India (1961) criminalized the giving and taking of dowry. Despite these laws, enforcement remains a challenge.
- **Grassroots Movements:** Grassroots movements and campaigns against dowry have gained momentum. These movements aim to raise awareness, change mindsets, and support victims of dowry-related violence.

The dowry system has a complex history, evolving from a voluntary provision for the bride's security to a compulsory demand that places immense financial and social pressure on families. While legal reforms and cultural shifts are challenging the practice, entrenched social norms and economic factors perpetuate it. Understanding its origins and evolution is crucial in formulating effective strategies to combat the dowry system and promote gender equality.

Impact of Dowry on Gender Equality:

The dowry system perpetuates gender inequality in various ways, and understanding these impacts can help in formulating strategies to promote gender equality. Here's an analysis of how the dowry system affects gender equality and steps to address these issues:

1. *Economic Burden on Families:*

The economic burden on families in the context of dowry refers to the financial strain placed on the bride's family due to the expectation of providing substantial gifts or payments to the groom's family during marriage. This burden often includes significant expenses such as cash, jewelry, household items, or property, which are demanded as part of traditional dowry practices in some cultures.

- **Financial Strain:** Dowry demands place a significant financial burden on the bride's family, often leading to debt and economic hardship. This perpetuates the perception of girls as financial liabilities.
- **Preference for Sons:** The economic strain encourages a preference for sons over daughters, leading to gender-biased practices such as sex-selective abortions and neglect of girl children.

2. *Reinforcement of Gender Roles:*

Reinforcement of Gender Roles in the context of dowry refers to the perpetuation or strengthening of traditional societal expectations and norms related to gender through the practice of giving or receiving dowry.

- **Dependency:** The dowry system reinforces the notion that women are dependent on men, as dowry is seen as compensation for the "burden" of taking care of the wife.
- **Subordination:** This system entrenches the subordinate status of women within the family and society, as they are often treated as commodities to be traded.

3. *Domestic Violence and Harassment:*

Domestic Violence and Harassment refers to any form of physical, emotional, sexual, or economic abuse inflicted upon a person (typically a woman) by her spouse or in-laws due to dissatisfaction with the dowry given at the time of marriage. It is a significant social issue in many cultures where dowry practices are prevalent.

- **Abuse:** Women who bring insufficient dowry may face domestic violence, harassment, and even murder. This creates an environment of fear and oppression.
- **Vulnerability:** The dowry system increases women's vulnerability to exploitation and abuse, undermining their dignity and self-worth.

4. Educational and Career Limitations:

Educational and Career Limitations refer to the constraints or obstacles imposed on a person's educational or career pursuits due to the pressures or expectations associated with dowry.

- **Reduced Investment:** Families may invest less in the education and career development of daughters, prioritizing saving for dowry instead. This limits women's opportunities for personal and professional growth.
- **Early Marriages:** The pressure to marry off daughters early to avoid higher dowry demands later discourages education and career aspirations for girls.

One of the primary benefits of rejecting dowry is the alleviation of financial burdens on families. The pressure to accumulate dowry can lead to excessive spending, loans, and even financial crises for the bride's family. By eliminating dowry demands, families can redirect their resources towards more productive investments, such as education and healthcare, thereby enhancing their financial stability and prospects.

Social and Economic Impact of Dowry on Families:

The dowry system has far-reaching effects on families, particularly on the bride's family, impacting them both economically and socially. Here's an analysis of these impacts:

1. Financial Burden:

It refers to the significant economic strain imposed on families due to the demands of dowry, often leading to debt, financial insecurity, and diminished quality of life.

- **Debt and Loans:** Many families incur significant debt to meet dowry demands, often taking out high-interest loans or selling assets. This debt can take years to repay, leading to long-term financial instability.
- **Reduced Savings:** The need to save for dowry can deplete family savings, leaving little or no financial buffer for emergencies or other important expenditures like healthcare and education.

2. Impact on Education:

It refers to how the practice of dowry affects access to and quality of education for individuals within affected families, often leading to limited educational opportunities, particularly for women.

- **Limited Investment in Education:** Families may prioritize saving for dowry over investing in the education of daughters, limiting their opportunities for personal and professional development.
- **Discontinuation of Studies:** Girls may be forced to discontinue their education early to get married and reduce the dowry amount, further perpetuating the cycle of dependency and economic disadvantage.

3. Economic Inequality:

It refers to the disparity in wealth and resources among families, exacerbated by dowry demands that financially burden less affluent families while enriching others.

- **Widening Gap:** The dowry system exacerbates economic inequality, with wealthier families being able to meet dowry demands more easily, while poorer families struggle, leading to a cycle of poverty and economic disparity.

4. Gender Discrimination:

Gender discrimination in the context of the social and economic impact of dowry on families refers to the unfair treatment and systemic disadvantage faced by women, perpetuated by the cultural practice of dowry, leading to financial burdens, limited opportunities, and social inequalities.

- **Preference for Sons:** The economic burden of dowry can lead to a preference for sons over daughters, resulting in gender-biased practices such as sex-selective abortions and neglect of girl children.
- **Devaluation of Women:** Women are often viewed as financial liabilities rather than assets, leading to discrimination and unequal treatment within the family and society.

5. Domestic Violence and Abuse:

It refers to the detrimental social and economic impacts of dowry on families.

- **Marital Abuse:** Women whose families cannot meet dowry demands often face harassment, abuse, and even violence from their in-laws. This abuse can range from verbal and emotional to physical, sometimes resulting in dowry deaths.
- **Mental Health Issues:** The pressure to provide dowry and the associated harassment can lead to severe mental health issues for women, including depression and anxiety.

6. Social Status:

Social status refers to the relative rank or standing of an individual or family within a society, often determined by factors such as wealth, occupation, education, and social connections.

- **Prestige and Reputation:** In many communities, the amount of dowry given or received is seen as a measure of social status and prestige. Families often feel pressured to meet or exceed social expectations to maintain or enhance their reputation, leading to competitive dowry practices.
- **Stigma and Ostracism:** Families unable to provide an adequate dowry may face social stigma and ostracism. This can lead to isolation and a

lower standing in the community, affecting their social interactions and support networks.

- **Marriage Prospects:** The dowry system can negatively affect the marriage prospects of women from families that cannot afford substantial dowries, leading to delays in marriage or difficulty finding suitable matches. This social pressure reinforces the cycle of dowry demands.

7. Impact on Family Dynamics:

The dowry system can strain family relationships, perpetuating conflict, inequality, and emotional stress.

- **Strained Relationships:** The financial burden and stress of fulfilling dowry demands can strain relationships within the bride's family. Parents and daughters may experience guilt, resentment, and tension, weakening family bonds.
- **Intra-Family Conflict:** Disputes over dowry can lead to conflicts within the extended family, disrupting family harmony and unity. These conflicts can persist and affect family relationships for generations.

8. Social Mobility:

The ability of individuals or families to move up or down the socioeconomic ladder is influenced by factors such as education, income, and social networks.

- **Hindrance to Progress:** The dowry system can act as a barrier to social mobility, especially for economically disadvantaged families. The financial strain and social stigma associated with dowry can prevent families from improving their socio-economic status.
- **Cycle of Poverty:** By prioritizing dowry over other essential investments like education and business opportunities, families can remain trapped in a cycle of poverty, with limited chances for upward mobility.

Dowry and Modernity: Changing Trends in Urban vs Rural Areas:

It can be understood as an exploration of how the practice and perception of dowry have evolved, particularly in the context of urban and rural settings.

Urban Areas:

Urban areas refer to cities or towns characterized by higher population density, advanced infrastructure, and greater economic activity compared to rural areas.

- **Economic Affluence:** In urban settings, families often have higher incomes and greater access to education and employment opportunities. This economic stability can reduce the emphasis on dowry as a financial transaction.
- **Education and Awareness:** Urban populations generally have higher levels of education and awareness about gender equality and legal rights. This awareness can lead to a more critical view of dowry practices.
- **Shift towards Gifts:** Instead of traditional dowry practices involving cash or assets, urban families may opt for symbolic gifts or contributions towards the couple's future, emphasizing personal and practical utility over financial exchange.

Rural Areas:

Rural areas refer to regions that are outside of urban centers, often characterized by lower population density, limited infrastructure, and a predominantly agricultural economy. In many countries, rural areas tend to have more traditional and conservative social structures, which can influence the prevalence and practices of dowry.

- **Economic Constraints:** Rural communities often face economic challenges, with limited income sources and higher levels of poverty. Dowry demands can exacerbate these challenges, leading to financial strain and debt for the bride's family.

- **Traditional Values:** Cultural and traditional values hold significant sway in rural areas, where dowry is often seen as a marker of family honor, status, and social validation.
- **Gender Norms:** Deep-rooted gender norms in rural settings may reinforce the perception of women as economic burdens, perpetuating dowry demands as a means to secure a daughter's marriage.

Role of Education in Eradicating Dowry:

Education is pivotal in transforming societal norms and eradicating harmful practices like the dowry system. Here's how education can contribute to changing mindsets and eliminating dowry:

1. Empowerment Through Knowledge:

It refers to equipping individuals with the awareness and skills needed to challenge and transform societal norms that perpetuate the dowry system.

- **Awareness of Rights:** Education helps individuals, especially women, understand their legal rights and the negative implications of dowry. Knowledge about laws prohibiting dowry can empower women to resist such demands.
- **Critical Thinking:** Educated individuals are more likely to question traditional practices and recognize the unjust nature of dowry, fostering a culture of critical thinking and reform.

2. Economic Independence:

Achieving financial self-sufficiency through education, enabling individuals to resist dowry practices, and promoting gender equality.

- **Financial Stability:** Education increases employment opportunities for women, leading to financial independence. Financially independent women are less likely to be seen as burdens, reducing the perceived necessity for dowry.

- **Valuing Skills over Dowry:** With education, the value of a person shifts from dowry contributions to personal skills and professional achievements, altering societal perceptions.

3. Changing Social Norms:

Education empowers individuals to challenge and transform traditional practices, such as dowry, fostering a society that values equality and human dignity.

- **Role Models:** Educated individuals can serve as role models, promoting marriages based on mutual respect and equality rather than financial transactions.
- **Raising Awareness:** Schools and colleges can be platforms for raising awareness about the harmful effects of dowry, encouraging students to pledge against this practice.

4. Promoting Gender Equality:

Promoting Gender Equality through education is crucial in eradicating dowry by fostering awareness, empowering women, and challenging societal norms.

- **Challenging Norms:** Education fosters gender equality by questioning societal norms that sustain the dowry system. It promotes equal treatment and opportunities for all genders.
- **Female Agency:** Educated women are more likely to assert their agency in marriage decisions, reducing the acceptance of dowry as a norm.

5. Curriculum and Policy Changes:

It refers to systematic revisions and implementations in educational content and regulations aimed at raising awareness, altering perceptions, and fostering attitudes that reject the dowry system.

- **Incorporating Social Issues:** Including topics on social issues like dowry in school curricula can sensitize young minds early on.
- **Policy Advocacy:** Educated individuals are better equipped to advocate for and implement policies that protect women's rights and promote equality, contributing to the eradication of dowry.

By fostering a culture of equality, awareness, and independence, education can play a critical role in eliminating the dowry system and promoting a more just and equitable society. Rejecting dowry fosters gender equality by valuing individuals based on their merits rather than their economic contributions. It encourages families to focus on qualities such as education, skills, and personal compatibility in marital arrangements, rather than perpetuating stereotypes and expectations tied to dowry. This shift empowers women to assert their worth beyond material considerations, promoting a more equitable society where all individuals are respected for their intrinsic value.

Case Studies of Dowry-Free Marriages:

Present some real-life examples of marriages that took place without any dowry and how these have been successful, serving as a model for others.

Case Study 1: The Story of Geet and Arjun

Geet and Arjun, both from educated families in Bangalore, decided to marry without any exchange of dowry. Both sets of parents supported their decision, emphasizing equality and mutual respect over financial transactions.

Implementation:

- **Equality and Respect:** Their wedding focused on celebrating their union rather than material exchanges. Guests were informed about the dowry-free nature of the wedding, promoting awareness.
- **Community Support:** The couple received widespread support from their community and used their platform to advocate against dowry practices.

Outcome:

- **Successful Marriage:** Geet and Arjun's marriage has been successful, built on mutual respect and shared responsibilities. They have become role models in their community.
- **Positive Influence:** Their decision inspired other couples and families to consider dowry-free marriages, contributing to a gradual shift in societal norms.

Case Study 2: Anu and Vishal's Progressive Union

Anu, an engineer, and Vishal, a software developer, met through mutual friends in Mumbai. Both had strong beliefs against dowry and agreed to a marriage free of such practices.

Implementation:

- **Simple Wedding:** Their wedding was a simple, low-cost affair focused on the presence of close family and friends. They emphasized their professional achievements and personal values over traditional dowry customs.
- **Media Coverage:** The couple shared their story on social media, gaining attention and sparking conversations about the harmful effects of dowry.

Outcome:

- **Career and Personal Growth:** Anu and Vishal continued to excel in their careers, unburdened by the financial strain often associated with dowry. Their partnership has thrived on equality and shared goals.
- **Community Engagement:** They have been active in community initiatives that educate people about the benefits of dowry-free marriages, encouraging others to follow their example.

The Impact of Dowry on a Financially Struggling Family:

Once upon a time, a financially weak family was living in a village. The family consisted of a man, his wife, a daughter, and a son. As time passed, the children grew older, but the family's financial condition remained the same because the only earning member was the father. All his earnings were spent on household expenses, school fees, tuition fees, and transportation, leaving no money to save.

Despite their financial struggles, the children were academically bright. The parents decided to invest in their children's education rather than saving money, hoping to secure their future. Over the years, both children secured good jobs with decent salaries, improving the family's financial condition somewhat. They weren't wealthy, but they were better off than before.

Eventually, people began discussing the daughter's marriage. However, the parents were reluctant, saying they couldn't afford it at the moment. Despite their protests, they were pressured into arranging her marriage. After finalizing the proposal, the mediator came to their house and asked how much dowry they would give. The girl's parents were shocked and argued that their educated, working daughter should be sufficient, so why should they give a dowry?

The mediator insisted that because the groom's family had a high financial status, giving dowry was a matter of respect. The parents, seeing that the match, groom, and his family were all good, decided to adjust their finances somehow to provide the dowry. They promised the mediator they would arrange a car, furniture, and some money.

The parents managed to gather everything before the wedding and gave the dowry. However, this left them in a worse financial condition than before. Previously, they had no debt, but now they were heavily in debt.

After the wedding, the daughter constantly worried about her family's financial stress, knowing they were now deep in debt because of the dowry. She offered to help with her salary, but her parents refused, saying they wouldn't take money from their daughter after marriage. Her father assured her that he and her brother would manage the debt and that she should focus on being happy in her new home.

Despite this, the daughter's stress grew, and she found it increasingly difficult to respect her husband and in-laws. Concerned, they took her to a psychiatrist, who revealed that her internal resentment toward her in-laws was growing. She wanted to respect them, but she couldn't because of the dowry issue. This strained her desire to continue the marriage.

Her parents were called in and tried to reassure her that they would handle the debt easily, but her well-being was their primary concern. Gradually, the daughter tries to settle down and adapt to her new family, finding some peace amid the upheaval. However, unable to adjust to her in-laws and husband, she decided to divorce after a year and returned to live with her parents. This is how their marriage ended with dowry as the only issue.

Insights Gained from this Story:

What can we learn from this story? In the narrative, the parents state that their daughter, being educated and employed, does not require a dowry. This suggests that they believe a dowry is necessary for daughters who are not working. However, this view is problematic. Both the bride and groom should be responsible for managing their household together. If the groom accepts a dowry to care for his bride, it raises the question of how he will provide for her throughout their entire life. Dowry should not be a consideration, regardless of whether the woman is employed or a housewife. If the husband works, the wife should manage the home; if both work, they should share both domestic and professional responsibilities.

Some argue that the practice of dowry will end if the bride's family stops giving it, but this is not true. The cessation of dowry can only occur if the groom's family chooses to end the practice. Bride's families often provide dowries to prevent their daughter from facing ridicule or harassment, sometimes even going into debt to fund elaborate weddings. Therefore, the resolution of the dowry issue relies on the groom's family.

If a groom refuses a dowry because of his self-confidence but later encounters financial difficulties such as business losses or health problems, he may accept assistance from the bride's family without compromising his self-respect. Such assistance should not be considered dowry but rather support during a time of need. The groom should regard the bride's parents with the same respect he would afford his own father. The key point is that dowry should not be a means to provide for the bride, but support given in times of need should be accepted without stigma.

Conclusion:

In conclusion, rejecting dowry brings about significant social benefits by reducing financial burdens on families, promoting gender equality, and advancing social justice and cultural progress. Embracing this shift requires collective effort and awareness-building within communities to challenge and ultimately transcend outdated practices that hinder societal development and equality. By rejecting dowry, societies can pave the way for a more just, equitable, and inclusive future for all individuals.

*"The chains of dowry are forged in tradition but can be broken by the courage of those who refuse to be bound. - **Satyam Tyagi**"*

8
Parenting and Family Dynamics

Parenting and Family Dynamics refers to the complex interactions and relationships within families, especially concerning the upbringing and nurturing of children. It encompasses various aspects such as parenting styles, roles and responsibilities of parents, communication patterns, discipline methods, and the impact of family structure on child development. Understanding family dynamics involves examining how parents influence their children's behavior, emotional development, and overall well-being, as well as how children, in turn, shape family interactions. Effective parenting fosters healthy relationships and provides a supportive environment crucial for a child's growth and development.

The Role of Communication in Family Relationships:

Communication is crucial in family relationships as it helps build trust, understanding, and strong bonds among family members. Effective communication involves:

- **Expressing Feelings and Needs:** Openly sharing emotions and needs helps family members understand and support each other better.
- **Active Listening:** Paying attention to what others say without interrupting shows respect and fosters a sense of being valued.
- **Resolving Conflicts:** Clear and calm communication can help resolve disagreements and prevent misunderstandings.

- **Building Trust:** Honest and transparent communication strengthens trust and reliability within the family.
- **Encouraging Support:** Sharing daily experiences and offering encouragement enhances emotional support and connection.

Good communication is key to maintaining healthy and happy family relationships, and promoting a supportive and loving environment for all members.

Balancing Work and Family Life: Challenges and Strategies:

There are some of the major **challenges** to balancing work and family life.

- **Time Management:** Juggling work responsibilities and family commitments can be overwhelming.
- **Stress and Burnout:** Constantly switching roles between work and home can lead to stress and exhaustion.
- **Quality Time:** Finding quality time to spend with family can be difficult with a busy work schedule.
- **Guilt:** Parents may feel guilty for not being able to fully dedicate themselves to either work or family.

These are some of the major **strategies** for balancing work and family life.

- **Set Priorities:** Identify what is most important and allocate time accordingly.
- **Create a Schedule:** Develop a daily or weekly plan that includes both work and family time.
- **Delegate Tasks:** Share responsibilities at home and work to reduce the burden.
- **Flexible Work Options:** Utilize flexible work hours or remote work opportunities if available.
- **Self-Care:** Take time for yourself to rest and recharge, which is crucial for maintaining balance.

Balancing work and family life requires careful planning, prioritization, and open communication. By implementing effective strategies, individuals can manage their responsibilities more efficiently and enjoy a healthier, more fulfilling life.

The Influence of Sibling Relationships on Personal Growth:

Sibling relationships play a significant role in shaping individuals' personal growth and development throughout their lives.

There are some of the **positive influences**:

- **Emotional Support**: Siblings can provide emotional support during challenging times, fostering resilience and empathy.
- **Social Skills Development**: Interacting with siblings teaches cooperation, negotiation, and conflict resolution skills.
- **Identity Formation**: Siblings help shape one's identity through shared experiences, values, and family dynamics.
- **Role Modeling**: Older siblings often serve as role models, influencing younger siblings' behaviors and aspirations.

There are some of the **challenges**:

- **Sibling Rivalry**: Competition and conflicts among siblings can lead to jealousy, resentment, and strained relationships.
- **Personality Differences**: Variations in personalities and interests can create misunderstandings and communication barriers.

The **impact on adult life** is as follows:

- **Lifelong Bonds**: Sibling relationships can provide enduring companionship and support in adulthood.
- **Family Dynamics**: Sibling interactions influence family dynamics, including decision-making and caregiving roles.

Overall, sibling relationships contribute significantly to personal growth by providing emotional support, social learning, and a sense of belonging. While challenges may arise, nurturing positive sibling connections can lead to lifelong benefits in individual development and family cohesion.

Single Parenting: Challenges and Solutions:

It refers to the experience of one parent raising a child or children alone. It presents challenges such as managing household responsibilities solo, balancing work and childcare, coping with financial pressures, and providing emotional support. Solutions include building a strong support network, accessing community resources for assistance, maintaining open communication with children, and prioritizing self-care to ensure both parent and child well-being.

Challenges of Single Parenting:

The challenges of single parenting encompass balancing responsibilities of childcare, finances, and personal well-being without the support of a partner.

- **Managing Household Responsibilities Alone:** Balancing chores, maintenance, and daily tasks without a partner's support.
- **Balancing Work and Childcare:** Juggling job responsibilities while ensuring adequate time and care for children.
- **Financial Pressures:** Handling expenses and providing for the family on a single income.
- **Emotional Support:** Providing emotional stability and guidance to children without another parent present.

Solutions for Single Parenting:

Solutions for single parenting encompass support systems and strategies to balance parental responsibilities effectively.

- **Building a Support Network:** Seeking help from family, friends, or support groups for practical and emotional assistance.
- **Open Communication with Children:** Maintaining honest and supportive dialogues to address challenges and foster a strong parent-child bond.

- **Prioritizing Self-Care:** Taking time for personal well-being and managing stress to maintain a healthy balance between parenting and personal life.

The Effects of Divorce on Children and Family Dynamics:

It explores how divorce impacts children and reshapes family relationships. It examines emotional, social, and psychological consequences for children, as well as changes in family structure and dynamics.

Effects on Children:

It refers to the of various factors such as environment, upbringing, and experiences on their development and well-being.

- **Emotional Impact:** Children may experience sadness, anger, or anxiety due to the disruption of family life.
- **Behavioral Changes:** Some children may exhibit behavioral issues or regress in development.
- **Academic Performance:** Divorce can affect children's academic performance and concentration in school.
- **Long-Term Effects:** There can be lasting effects on self-esteem, relationships, and future emotional stability.

Family Dynamics:

It refers to the patterns of interactions, relationships, and roles within a family unit.

- **Parent-Child Relationships:** Divorce can alter parent-child relationships, affecting communication and support.
- **Co-Parenting Challenges:** Coordinating parenting responsibilities post-divorce can be challenging but crucial for children's well-being.
- **Financial Strain:** Divorce often leads to financial adjustments that impact family dynamics and lifestyle.
- **Remarriage and Blended Families:** Introducing new partners and blending families can further complicate family dynamics.

Understanding the effects of divorce on children and family dynamics underscores the importance of emotional support, stability, and effective communication. While divorce brings challenges, support systems can help families navigate this transition and promote children's well-being.

Impact of Parenting Styles on Child Development:

Parenting styles affect how children grow and develop in terms of behavior, emotions, and social skills. There are four main parenting styles:

1. Authoritative: (Supportive and Firm)

A leadership style that combines guidance with encouragement and unwavering decision-making.

- **Description:** Parents are supportive and set clear rules.
- **Effect:** Children are confident, responsible, and good with others.

2. Authoritarian: (Strict and Controlling)

It is characterized by strict control and adherence to authority, often with limited individual freedom or input.

- **Description:** Parents are strict and expect obedience.
- **Effect:** Children may follow rules but can be anxious and have lower self-esteem.

3. Permissive: (Lenient and Indulgent)

It is characterized by being lenient and indulgent, allowing freedom and flexibility.

- **Description:** Parents are lenient and set few rules.
- **Effect:** Children may have trouble with self-discipline and respecting authority.

4. Neglectful: (Uninvolved and Indifferent)

It is characterized by being uninvolved and indifferent towards responsibilities or relationships.

- **Description:** Parents are uninvolved and show little interest.
- **Effect:** Children may struggle with attachment, school, and self-worth.

Balanced parenting, especially the authoritative style, tends to produce the best outcomes, helping children to be emotionally stable, socially skilled, and successful in school.

Helicopter Parenting vs. Free-Range Parenting: Pros and Cons:

Helicopter parenting involves over-involvement in a child's life, while free-range parenting emphasizes independence with less parental oversight; each approach has benefits and drawbacks impacting child development.

Helicopter Parenting:

Helicopter parenting is a style where parents are highly involved in their children's lives, often overseeing and managing many aspects of their daily activities, education, and social interactions. They tend to hover over their children, hence the term "helicopter."

Pros:

- **Safety and Protection:** Children are closely monitored, reducing the risk of accidents or exposure to harmful situations.
- **Academic Success:** Parents' involvement can lead to better academic performance due to constant supervision and support.
- **Strong Parental Bond:** Close involvement can foster strong emotional bonds between parents and children.

Cons:

- **Lack of Independence:** Children may struggle to develop autonomy and decision-making skills as they rely heavily on their parents.
- **Anxiety and Stress:** Over-involvement can lead to increased anxiety and stress in children who may feel pressured to meet high expectations.
- **Reduced Problem-Solving Skills:** Children may not learn to handle challenges or failures independently, impacting their resilience.

Free-Range Parenting:

Free-range parenting emphasizes giving children more freedom to explore and make their own decisions with minimal parental intervention. This approach trusts children to learn from their experiences and promotes independence.

Pros:

- **Independence and Responsibility:** Children learn to make decisions and take responsibility for their actions, fostering independence.
- **Problem-Solving Skills:** By facing challenges on their own, children develop critical thinking and problem-solving abilities.
- **Confidence and Self-Esteem:** Autonomy and trust from parents can boost children's confidence and self-esteem.

Cons:

- **Safety Concerns:** Children may be more exposed to risks and potentially dangerous situations with less supervision.
- **Judgment from Others:** Free-range parenting can be misunderstood and criticized by others who believe it is neglectful.
- **Potential for Failure:** Children might face significant failures or setbacks without parental guidance, which can be challenging to navigate alone.

Both helicopter parenting and free-range parenting have their advantages and disadvantages. The key is finding a balance that ensures children's safety and well-being while promoting their independence and personal growth. Effective parenting often involves adapting strategies to suit the child's needs, personality, and developmental stage.

Grandparents as Primary Caregivers: Benefits and Challenges:

Grandparents taking on the role of primary caregivers for their grandchildren is a significant family dynamic shaped by both benefits and challenges. On the positive side, grandparents provide stability during times of family crisis, offering a nurturing environment steeped in unconditional love and wisdom derived from their life experiences. Their presence often ensures continuity in upbringing, preserving family traditions and values that contribute to a child's sense of identity and security. Financially, grandparents frequently contribute, easing the financial strain on parents and ensuring adequate resources for the grandchildren's needs.

However, this caregiving role is not without its difficulties. Aging grandparents may encounter health challenges that affect their ability to keep up with the physical demands of childcare. Socially, they may experience isolation or reduced engagement in community activities due to the responsibilities of caregiving. Legal complexities can arise when formalizing custody or guardianship, necessitating legal interventions to secure the best interests of the children.

To navigate these challenges, family support is crucial. Open communication among family members facilitates the sharing of responsibilities and provides emotional and practical assistance to grandparents. Community resources such as support groups and respite care services offer valuable support, allowing grandparents to take breaks and maintain their well-being. Prioritizing self-care is essential for grandparents, ensuring they have the physical and emotional strength to fulfill their caregiving duties effectively.

In conclusion, grandparents serving as primary caregivers play a vital role in the lives of their grandchildren, providing love, stability, and continuity. While they face challenges related to health, social isolation, and legal issues, proactive support from family and community resources can help mitigate these challenges. Recognizing and supporting grandparents in their caregiving role strengthens family bonds and promotes the well-being of both generations involved.

> "*Some of you may be fortunate to have experienced the love of grandparents. Times have changed, and fewer people are able to spend their lives with grandparents for various reasons. Perhaps parents have moved away due to jobs, or the high mortality rate has taken grandparents away at the age of 50-60. Health issues may also keep them occupied. However, it's a wonderful feeling if you have ever felt their love. So please try to get in touch with your grandparents; they care about you the most and think about your well-being more than anyone else.*"

Cultural Differences in Parenting Practices:

It explores how parenting methods can differ between cultures. It shows how beliefs, traditions, and what society expects can affect how parents raise their children. These differences influence how kids behave, learn, and grow up in their own culture. Recognizing these variations helps people understand and respect different ways of parenting, fostering better understanding and communication between cultures.

> *"Have you ever heard the saying that children learn by example? Whatever they are taught, they learn the same way. Whatever they see people doing around them, they learn those things too. They follow the culture or traditions they observe and learn everything from that. For example, if you take care of your parents, your children will likely take care of you in the future. However, if you don't show respect to your parents, your children might do the same to you later on. Therefore, pay attention to yourself because the younger generation is watching and learning from you."*

Managing Conflict in Family Relationships:

It is essential for maintaining harmony and fostering healthy interactions among family members. In every family, conflicts inevitably arise due to differences in personalities, opinions, values, and expectations. These conflicts can range from minor disagreements to more significant disputes that impact relationships and the overall family dynamics.

Effective conflict management in family settings involves several key strategies. Firstly, open and respectful communication is crucial. Family members should express their thoughts and feelings honestly while actively listening to each other without interruptions. This promotes understanding and helps in finding common ground or compromises.

Secondly, empathy plays a vital role in conflict resolution. Understanding each other's perspectives and emotions allows family members to approach disagreements with compassion and sensitivity. This helps in de-escalating tensions and preventing conflicts from escalating further.

Thirdly, setting clear boundaries and expectations can prevent misunderstandings and reduce conflict. Establishing ground rules for communication and behavior within the family helps in managing expectations and promoting mutual respect.

Moreover, Families can brainstorm solutions together, evaluate different options, and agree on compromises that address everyone's needs and concerns. This collaborative approach fosters a sense of teamwork and reinforces family unity.

Additionally, managing conflict in family relationships requires patience and forgiveness. It's important to recognize that conflicts are a natural part of relationships and that resolving them requires time and effort. Forgiving past grievances and focusing on moving forward can strengthen bonds and promote healing within the family.

Lastly, seeking outside support or professional help may be necessary for resolving deep-seated conflicts or when communication within the family becomes challenging. Family counseling or mediation can provide unbiased guidance and facilitate constructive dialogue.

In conclusion, effectively managing conflict in family relationships involves open communication, empathy, setting boundaries, problem-solving, patience, and seeking outside support when needed. By addressing conflicts positively and proactively, families can cultivate stronger bonds, mutual respect, and a supportive environment for everyone involved.

"Family is not an important thing, it's everything. - **Michael J. Fox***"*

The Impact of Technology on Family Interactions:

It examines how digital devices and online platforms influence communication and relationships within families. It explores both the positive and negative effects of technology on familial dynamics.

These are some of the **positive impacts** of technology on family interactions.

- **Enhanced Communication:** Facilitates instant communication through messaging apps, video calls, and social media, bridging geographical distances.

- **Convenience:** Simplifies coordination of family schedules, sharing of information, and access to educational resources.
- **Bonding Opportunities:** Enables shared activities such as online gaming, streaming movies, and participating in virtual family events.

These are some of the **negative impacts** of technology on family interactions.

- **Decreased Face-to-Face Interaction:** Reduces in-person conversations and quality time spent together, potentially weakening emotional bonds.
- **Distraction and Overuse:** This leads to family members spending excessive time on screens, detracting from meaningful interactions.
- **Privacy Concerns:** Raises issues around digital privacy, cyberbullying, and exposure to inappropriate content.

Managing Technology Use:

This is how we can use the limited technology and manage family dynamics.

- **Setting Boundaries:** Establishing screen-free times or zones to prioritize face-to-face interactions.
- **Educating About Risks:** Discuss online safety, digital etiquette, and responsible use of technology within the family.
- **Balancing Use:** Encouraging a healthy balance between online and offline activities to promote well-being and family connection.

Understanding the impact of technology on family interactions helps families navigate its effects proactively. By leveraging its benefits while managing its drawbacks, families can foster meaningful connections, communication, and harmony in an increasingly digital world.

"*As you are aware, in today's world, our parents often engage with news and conversations, while our generation is deeply immersed in mobile chats, games, and similar activities. This shift makes it challenging for younger generations to spend quality time with their parents. Have you ever considered how parents might feel upon realizing that their children are more interested in their online friends than in spending time with them? This trend is already noticeable, and it's possible that future generations might continue in the same vein. Both parents and children could become increasingly engrossed in their phones, leading to diminished family interactions and strained relationships. This situation could ultimately erode the love and respect within families."*

Raising Emotionally Intelligent Children:

Raising emotionally intelligent children is crucial for their overall development and well-being. It involves nurturing their ability to understand and manage emotions effectively from a young age.

Parents play a pivotal role in this process by modeling healthy emotional behaviors and creating a supportive environment where children feel safe expressing their feelings. By teaching children to recognize and label their emotions, parents help them develop emotional awareness. This awareness extends to understanding the emotions of others, fostering empathy and compassion.

Emotion regulation is another essential aspect of emotional intelligence. Children learn strategies to cope with strong emotions, such as taking deep breaths or using calming techniques. This ability not only helps in managing stress but also enhances their resilience in facing challenges.

Empathy, a cornerstone of emotional intelligence, enables children to relate to others' feelings and perspectives. Parents encourage empathy by discussing diverse emotions and encouraging their children to consider how others might feel in different situations. Social skills are also cultivated through emotional intelligence. These skills enable children to build positive relationships with peers and adults, contributing to their social development.

Emotionally intelligent children are more likely to succeed academically as well. They exhibit better concentration, motivation, and problem-solving abilities, which are essential for learning and academic achievement.

Parents can support their children's emotional intelligence by providing guidance and encouragement. They create opportunities for open communication, where children feel comfortable discussing their feelings and seeking support when needed. By reinforcing positive behaviors and acknowledging efforts, parents help build their children's self-esteem and confidence in managing emotions.

In conclusion, raising emotionally intelligent children involves fostering emotional awareness, regulation, empathy, and social skills. This holistic approach equips children with essential tools to navigate life's challenges, build meaningful relationships, and thrive academically and emotionally. By investing in their emotional development, parents set the stage for their children's lifelong well-being and success.

"As you are aware, emotional insight can often guide us to make the most effective decisions in life. Without emotions, you might find it easier to make quick decisions that could lead to significant financial gain. However, if you are guided by emotions, you may face some career setbacks due to your decision-making process. Despite this, you are likely to find greater personal satisfaction with these choices, as decisions made from the heart tend to bring deeper happiness."

The Role of Fathers in Modern Parenting:

In modern parenting, the role of fathers has undergone significant evolution, moving beyond traditional stereotypes of being primary to becoming more actively involved in all aspects of their children's lives. Today, fathers are increasingly recognized for their crucial role in nurturing, supporting, and shaping their children's development.

Emotionally, fathers play a vital role in providing stability and encouragement. They contribute to their children's emotional well-being by offering guidance, comfort, and a sense of security. This emotional support helps children develop confidence, resilience, and healthy self-esteem as they navigate life's challenges.

Practically, modern fathers are more hands-on in parenting than ever before. They participate in daily caregiving tasks such as feeding, bathing, and playing with their children. This active involvement not only strengthens the bond between father and child but also promotes a deeper understanding and connection.

Fathers also serve as role models for their children, demonstrating important values, behaviors, and problem-solving skills. By showcasing respect, responsibility, and compassion in their interactions with family members, fathers instill these qualities in their children, shaping their moral development and character.

In terms of co-parenting, modern fathers collaborate with mothers in decision-making, discipline strategies, and establishing family routines. This partnership fosters a balanced approach to parenting, ensuring that both parents contribute equally to their children's upbringing and well-being.

Educationally, involved fathers support their children's academic achievements by taking an active interest in their schooling. They attend parent-teacher meetings, help with homework, and encourage a love for learning. This engagement not only boosts academic performance but also demonstrates the importance of education and lifelong learning.

Financially, fathers provide for their families while also balancing their responsibilities at home. This dual role showcases a commitment to both providing for and nurturing their children, emphasizing the importance of shared responsibilities within the family unit.

The impact of active fatherhood is profound and far-reaching. *Research shows that children with involved fathers tend to exhibit better social skills, academic success, and emotional well-being.* They are more likely to form positive relationships, exhibit empathy, and handle stress effectively. This inclusive approach not only benefits children but also enhances marital relationships and contributes to overall family stability.

In conclusion, the role of fathers in modern parenting is characterized by emotional support, hands-on involvement, positive role modeling, collaborative co-parenting, educational engagement, and financial responsibility. Recognizing and promoting active fatherhood is crucial for nurturing healthy, well-rounded children and fostering strong, resilient families in today's dynamic and evolving societal landscape.

> *"I am focusing specifically on fathers rather than mothers because, historically, children—regardless of gender—have always felt more comfortable expressing themselves openly to their mothers. This emotional connection is deeply rooted and does not require modern intervention or beyond tradition. However, traditionally, children often felt more reserved in their interactions with their fathers, and this dynamic persists in some cases today. Consequently, I have chosen to emphasize this particular aspect to address the ongoing issues of bonding and communication between fathers and their children."*

The Importance of Parental Involvement in Education:

Parental involvement in education is crucial for the academic success and overall development of children. It refers to the active participation of parents in their children's learning experiences, both at home and at school.

Parental involvement in education plays a pivotal role in fostering a child's academic achievement, social development, and overall well-being. By actively engaging in their children's education, parents create a supportive environment that empowers students to thrive academically and personally. Recognizing and encouraging parental involvement is essential for building strong partnerships between home and school, ultimately benefiting the educational outcomes of children.

*"It is not what you do for your children, but what you have taught them to do for themselves that will make them successful human beings. - **Ann Landers**"*

The Role of Extended Family in Child Rearing:

In today's times, joint families face challenges that can impact their success. While there are many benefits to living in a joint family, such as emotional support, shared responsibilities, and a strong sense of community, there are also some drawbacks that need to be considered:

- **Conflict Resolution:** Differences in opinions and lifestyles among family members can lead to conflicts that are sometimes difficult to resolve. Disputes over financial matters, child-rearing practices, or personal boundaries can strain relationships.
- **Privacy and Space:** Living near extended family members may limit individual privacy and personal space. Lack of personal space can sometimes lead to feelings of frustration or the need for personal independence.
- **Dependency Issues:** In some cases, family members may become overly dependent on each other, leading to issues of control or interference in personal decisions. This can affect individual autonomy and decision-making.

- **Generational Differences:** Generation gaps in attitudes, beliefs, and values can sometimes lead to misunderstandings or conflicts regarding modern versus traditional practices, especially concerning child-rearing, education, or career choices.
- **Financial Burdens:** Sharing finances and resources can sometimes lead to financial strain if there is inequality in income or differing financial priorities among family members. Disparities in financial contributions or expectations can cause tension.
- **Individual Growth:** In a joint family, individuals may find it challenging to pursue personal goals or career aspirations independently. The need to consider family expectations or opinions in decision-making can sometimes limit individual growth or opportunities.

Despite these challenges, successful joint families often thrive through effective communication, mutual respect, and a shared commitment to resolving conflicts. By addressing potential drawbacks proactively and maintaining an open dialogue, joint families can harness their strengths while mitigating the challenges, thereby fostering a harmonious and supportive family environment.

> *"Living in a joint family presents both advantages and challenges. It is essential to acknowledge the potential disadvantages associated with this arrangement. To foster positive relationships and minimize daily conflicts while pursuing personal goals, it may be beneficial to maintain some degree of distance from family members. This does not imply that joint family living is inherently negative; rather, its success largely depends on the family dynamics. If family members respect each other's decisions and maintain mutual respect, a joint family can be advantageous. However, if this respect is lacking, it may not be necessary for every generation to cohabit. In such cases, living separately might be a prudent choice for all involved."*

Mental Health and Parenting: Supporting Parents and Children:

Parenting plays a crucial role in the mental health and well-being of both parents and children. It involves the emotional, psychological, and social aspects of raising children in a nurturing and supportive environment.

- **Parental Mental Health Impact:** Parental mental health significantly influences parenting abilities. Mentally healthy parents can provide better emotional support, stability, and guidance to their children.
- **Child Mental Health:** A supportive parenting environment is crucial for children's mental health development. It helps build resilience, self-esteem, and emotional regulation skills.
- **Challenges Faced:** Parents may face challenges such as stress, anxiety, or depression, which can affect their ability to parent effectively. These challenges can arise from various sources, including work-life balance, financial stress, or personal issues.
- **Seeking Help:** It's important for parents to recognize when they need support and to seek help from mental health professionals or support groups. Addressing mental health challenges early can prevent negative impacts on both parents and children.

Supporting parental mental health is essential for creating a nurturing environment that promotes positive child development. By prioritizing mental well-being and seeking appropriate support, parents can effectively navigate challenges and provide a supportive foundation for their children's emotional and psychological growth. This holistic approach helps foster resilience, healthy relationships, and overall well-being within the family unit.

Blended Families: Navigating New Family Dynamics:

Blended families, also known as stepfamilies, form when parents with children from previous relationships come together. Blended families are formed when parents with children from previous marriages or relationships get married or start living together.

These families involve a mix of biological children, stepchildren, and sometimes half-siblings. This can create complex relationships and dynamics within the household.

These families face unique challenges such as complex relationships, loyalty conflicts, and differing parenting styles. An adjustment period is common as new family members learn to live together. Effective communication, mutual respect, and support from counseling or support groups can help overcome these challenges. With patience and effort, blended families can develop strong bonds, providing love, support, and a sense of belonging to all members.

Adoption: Building Strong Family Bonds:

Adoption and foster care are ways to build strong family bonds by providing children with loving, stable homes when they cannot stay with their biological families.

Adoption:

Adoption is the legal and social process through which individuals or couples assume parental responsibility for a child who is not biologically theirs.

- **Permanent Placement:** Adoption offers a permanent home to children, creating lifelong family bonds.
- **Emotional Support:** Adoptive families provide emotional security, love, and support, helping children feel valued and cherished.
- **Legal and Social Integration:** Adopted children gain the same legal rights as biological children, becoming integral parts of their new families.

Building Strong Family Bonds:

Building strong family bonds involves nurturing deep connections, fostering trust, and prioritizing meaningful interactions within the family unit.

- **Attachment and Trust:** Adoptive families focus on building attachment and trust, essential for healthy emotional development.
- **Consistency and Care:** Consistent care, nurturing, and positive interactions help children feel secure and form strong family connections.
- **Inclusive Family Dynamics:** Families that embrace openness, communication, and inclusivity help children adapt and feel accepted.

Adoption plays a crucial role in creating strong family bonds by providing children with the love, stability, and support they need. Whether through permanent adoption or temporary foster care, these families offer children the opportunity to thrive in a nurturing environment, building lasting, meaningful relationships.

Embracing Parenthood Together:

Pregnancy is a transformative journey that both partners should navigate together. Modern couples are redefining traditional roles by actively supporting each other through the pregnancy process. By sharing responsibilities and offering emotional support, partners not only enhance the well-being of the expectant mother but also strengthen their relationship and prepare for co-parenting. Embracing parenthood as a unified team fosters a deeper bond and a more balanced approach to raising a child.

Aarav and Meera had always been the perfect team. They met in college, where their shared sense of humor and mutual respect blossomed into a deep love. As they prepared to welcome their first child, they knew this journey would test their partnership in new ways. To prepare for their first child, they first consulted with their doctor to ensure that they were ready for childbirth.

When Meera became pregnant, the excitement was palpable, but so were the challenges. Meera struggled with morning sickness and fatigue, and Aarav saw firsthand the physical and emotional toll pregnancy took on her. Rather than staying on the sidelines, Aarav chose to be fully involved. He attended every prenatal appointment, read up on pregnancy and childbirth, and learned how to cook nutritious meals to support Meera's changing needs.

One evening, as Meera lay exhausted on the couch, Aarav took over the household chores, cleaned up after dinner, and gently rubbed her aching feet. Meera, overwhelmed by the tenderness and care, realized how much Aarav's support meant to her. They talked openly about their fears and hopes for their future as parents, finding comfort in their shared commitment to each other.

When the day of the delivery arrived, Aarav was by Meera's side, holding her hand and offering words of encouragement. During labor, his calm presence and unwavering support were a beacon of strength. As they welcomed their baby into the world, their bond was solidified by this shared experience of creating and nurturing new life.

The journey wasn't without its difficulties. Sleepless nights and the demands of a newborn tested their patience. They created a schedule for nighttime baby care so that while one of them slept, the other would stay awake and keep watch. Yet, Aarav and Meera continued to face these challenges as a team. They took turns caring for the baby, supported each other through the inevitable exhaustion, and celebrated the small victories together.

Their experience demonstrated the power of embracing parenthood together. By sharing the responsibilities and supporting each other, Aarav and Meera not only strengthened their relationship but also created a loving, balanced environment for their child. Their story is a testament to how a unified approach to parenting can transform challenges into opportunities for deeper connection and mutual growth.

Respect and Unity: The Sharma Family's Secret to Happiness:

In a small village lived Mr. and Mrs. Sharma with their three children, Aarav, Priya, and Aditi. They were a below-middle-class family, with just enough to eat and wear but not much else to spend. However, their neighbors were always shocked to see that despite their limited means, the Sharma household never seemed to have any arguments, unlike the wealthier families nearby who had cars and money but constant fights.

One day, the village head invited Mr. Sharma to his house for a meeting where 10-15 people were discussing contributing money to build a new road. Mr. Sharma said he would need to discuss it with his wife and children first. The villagers mocked him, calling him a slave to his wife and questioning why he needed to consult his children.

Mr. Sharma explained, "People often ask me why there are no fights in our house. It's because we respect each other so much that we make all decisions together, including financial ones. Even if it's just 100 rupees, we discuss it so everyone knows how much money we have and what we can spend. When Aarav was younger, he used to demand things without understanding, but now he discusses his needs with us and only asks for what we can afford. That's why we live happily together."

He continued, "I never force my children to study, but I do explain the importance of education so they understand."

The villagers, steeped in old traditions, didn't fully grasp his point about involving women and children in decision-making. This continued for years until

Mr. Sharma moved his family to the city. There, he worked hard and educated his children, who eventually settled into well-paying jobs. Their family dynamic remained the same, with every decision being made collectively.

People began to praise Mr. Sharma, noting they'd never seen a family like his. Even wealthy families who valued education started bringing their children to meet the Sharmas, hoping they would learn from their values. They would say, "Mr. Sharma, seeing your family makes us believe that everyone should live like this."

Mr. Sharma's children respected him immensely, not just because he consulted them on everything, but because they saw how much their father & mother respected their mother and mother-in-law respectively when she was alive. Children tend to emulate what they see, and by observing Mr. Sharma, his children learn to respect their parents. Always remember, if someone doesn't respect their parents, their children are unlikely to respect them either.

In the end, it's often said that money can't buy happiness. Happiness is created through an environment of mutual respect and understanding, where conflicts don't arise because everyone values and listens to each other.

"Call it a clan, call it a network, call it a tribe, call it a family. Whatever you call it, whoever you are, you need one. - **Jane Howard** *"*

9

Conflict and Resolution

Conflict is inevitable in life, but how we handle it defines us. We explore strategies for resolving disputes peacefully, fostering understanding and reconciliation in our relationships. Conflict is inevitable in human interaction, arising from differences in opinions, values, needs, or interests. Effective resolution of conflicts is crucial for maintaining harmony and fostering growth in personal, professional, and societal contexts.

Types of Conflict:

These are the different types of conflicts:

- **Interpersonal Conflict:** Occurs between individuals due to personal differences, misunderstandings, or competition.
- **Intrapersonal Conflict:** Internal struggle within an individual, often involving dilemmas or emotional stress.
- **Organizational Conflict:** Arises in workplaces due to differing goals, resource allocation, or leadership styles.
- **Intergroup Conflict:** Occurs between different groups or teams, often due to competition or incompatible goals.
- **International Conflict:** Involves disputes between nations, typically over political, economic, or territorial issues.

Causes of Conflict:

These are the different causes of conflicts:

- **Communication Breakdown:** Miscommunication or lack of communication can lead to misunderstandings and conflict.
- **Divergent Goals and Interests:** Conflicts often arise when parties have different objectives or interests.
- **Value Differences:** Differing beliefs and values can lead to disagreements.
- **Resource Scarcity:** Competition over limited resources, such as time, money, or materials, can create conflict.
- **Power Imbalances:** Unequal power dynamics can lead to conflicts, especially when one party feels marginalized.

Conflict Resolution Strategies:

There are some of the strategies for conflict resolution.

- **Negotiation:** A process where parties discuss their differences and work towards a mutually acceptable solution.
- **Mediation:** Involves a neutral third party who helps facilitate a resolution between conflicting parties.
- **Arbitration:** A neutral third party makes a binding decision to resolve the conflict.
- **Collaboration:** Parties work together to find a win-win solution that satisfies everyone's needs.
- **Compromise:** Each party gives up something to reach a middle ground.
- **Avoidance:** Deliberately ignoring or withdrawing from the conflict, which can be useful for trivial issues but may not resolve underlying problems.
- **Accommodation:** One party yields to the other's demands, often used when the issue is more important to one party than the other.

Steps in Conflict Resolution:

Look at some of the steps that can be taken for conflict resolution.

- **Identify the Source:** Understand the root cause of the conflict.
- **Understand Perspectives:** Acknowledge the views and concerns of all parties involved.
- **Communicate Effectively:** Open, honest, and respectful communication is essential.
- **Brainstorm Solutions:** Collaboratively generate possible solutions.
- **Evaluate and Select:** Assess the potential solutions and agree on the best course of action.
- **Implement and Follow-Up:** Put the chosen solution into practice and monitor its effectiveness.

Effective conflict resolution is key to maintaining healthy relationships and productive environments. By understanding the types, causes, and strategies for resolving conflicts, individuals and organizations can navigate disagreements constructively, leading to positive outcomes and stronger connections.

"*In today's fast-paced world, it's common to see conflicts arising from various aspects of life, such as property disputes, romantic relationships, academic achievements, and other seemingly small issues. These conflicts often lead to unnecessary stress, broken relationships, and a general sense of discontent.*

For instance, families may argue over the division of inherited property, causing rifts that last for years. Friends may fall out over misunderstandings related to romantic interests, or students may feel intense pressure and jealousy over academic grades. These disagreements, though often rooted in small misunderstandings or personal insecurities, can escalate quickly, leading to long-term damage to relationships and personal well-being.

It's crucial to step back and recognize that these conflicts, while they may seem significant at the moment, are minor in the grand scheme of life. Prioritizing love, compassion, and understanding over material possessions or temporary achievements can lead to a more harmonious and fulfilling life.

By fostering open communication, empathy, and mutual respect, we can resolve disputes amicably and strengthen our relationships. Instead of focusing on what divides us, we should embrace what unites us: the shared human experience of love, joy, and connection. This shift in perspective can help us live more peacefully, appreciating the true value of our relationships and the simple joys of life.

In essence, by choosing love and harmony over conflict, we can create a more positive and supportive environment for ourselves and those around us. This approach not only enhances our happiness but also contributes to a more compassionate and cohesive society. "

Conflict and Resolution: A Heartfelt Approach

Conflict is a part of life, arising from differences in opinions, values, and needs. How we handle these conflicts can define our relationships and our personal growth. Here's a story that delves into the emotional depths of conflict and resolution.

The Story of Aisha and Meera:

Aisha and Meera have been inseparable friends since childhood. They shared dreams, fears, and countless memories. However, as they grew older, their paths began to diverge. Aisha, the daughter of a small-town teacher, dreamed of becoming a writer. Meera, coming from a wealthy family, aspired to take over her family's business.

The Conflict:

As their careers progressed, Aisha and Meera found less time for each other. Aisha struggled financially, pouring her heart into her stories, while Meera was often busy with meetings and business trips. Their differences began to create a rift. One day, during a heated argument, Meera accused Aisha of being irresponsible and chasing unrealistic dreams. Aisha, hurt and angry, accused Meera of forgetting the value of true friendship in her pursuit of wealth.

The Turning Point:

Months passed without a word between them. Both felt the pain of losing their friendship but were too proud to reach out. Then, one day, Aisha received an unexpected call from Meera's mother. Meera had met with an accident and was in the hospital. Without a second thought, Aisha rushed to her side.

Seeing Meera lying there, vulnerable and in pain, Aisha realized how trivial their conflicts were compared to the bond they shared. Meera, waking up to find Aisha holding her hand, felt a surge of relief and regret.

The Resolution:

Their reunion in the hospital room was filled with tears and heartfelt conversations. Aisha apologized for her harsh words, understanding the pressures Meera faced. Meera, in turn, expressed her admiration for Aisha's courage to follow her dreams and apologized for her insensitivity.

Communication: They realized the importance of honest communication. Instead of letting misunderstandings fester, they promised to talk openly about their feelings and struggles.

Empathy: Both learned to see things from the other's perspective. Meera began to appreciate the beauty in Aisha's writing, while Aisha understood the responsibilities weighing on Meera.

Support: They decided to support each other unconditionally. Meera used her business acumen to help Aisha publish her book, while Aisha's stories brought Meera a sense of peace and balance.

Conclusion:

Aisha and Meera's story shows that conflicts, though painful, can lead to deeper understanding and stronger bonds if resolved with empathy and love. In the end, it's the willingness to understand and support each other that truly matters, reminding us that our relationships are far more valuable than our differences.

The Importance of Communication in Relationships:

In any relationship, be it friendship, love, marriage, or family, communication is the key to understanding and resolving conflicts. A lack of communication can lead to misunderstandings and prolonged issues, while open dialogue fosters connection and mutual respect.

The Story of Aisha and Meera:

Consider the story of Aisha and Meera. Do you think their friendship was mended solely because of Meera's accident? No, it wasn't just the accident. The real turning point was their interaction in the hospital due to which they talked to each other. If they had communicated earlier, they might have resolved their issues sooner.

Why Communication Matters:

Effective communication is crucial in conflict resolution as it fosters understanding, reduces misunderstandings, and facilitates the negotiation of mutually acceptable solutions.

- **Prevents Misunderstandings:** Regular communication helps clarify intentions, thoughts, and feelings. Without it, assumptions can lead to unnecessary conflicts.
- **Builds Trust:** Open and honest conversations create a foundation of trust, making it easier to share vulnerabilities and rely on each other.
- **Strengthens Bonds:** Sharing experiences, whether they are challenges or triumphs, deepens connections and strengthens relationships.
- **Facilitates Problem-Solving:** Discussing issues openly allows for collaborative problem-solving, ensuring that both parties feel heard and valued.

Real-Life Applications:

Practical strategies and tools used to address and resolve disputes in everyday situations, fostering understanding and cooperation.

- **Friendship:** In friendships, regular catch-ups and heart-to-heart conversations help friends stay connected despite busy schedules. Just like Aisha and Meera could have resolved their differences sooner, friends should strive to communicate openly before misunderstandings grow.
- **Love and Marriage:** In romantic relationships, expressing feelings, discussing plans, and addressing conflicts directly are crucial. Miscommunications can lead to resentment, but clear communication fosters a healthy and supportive partnership.
- **Family:** Within families, open dialogue among members helps in understanding each other's perspectives and needs. It ensures that issues are resolved in a nurturing environment, promoting familial harmony.

Conclusion:

The story of Aisha and Meera teaches us a valuable lesson: communication is the lifeline of any relationship. Their friendship was rekindled not merely due to the accident, but because they finally had the chance to talk. By prioritizing communication, we can prevent misunderstandings, build trust, and strengthen our bonds. Whether it's friendship, love, marriage, or family, open and honest communication is the key to lasting and meaningful relationships.

*"The best way to resolve any problem in the human world is for all sides to sit down and talk. - **Dalai Lama**"*

10

Work-Life Integration

Work-Life Integration is an approach that aims to blend personal and professional responsibilities seamlessly, rather than treating them as separate domains that need to be balanced. This concept recognizes that work and life are interconnected and encourages individuals to find ways to harmonize these aspects to improve overall well-being and productivity. Achieving balance in life is essential for overall well-being. We explore strategies for integrating work and personal life harmoniously, ensuring fulfillment and success on your terms.

- **Flexibility:** Adopting flexible work hours and environments to accommodate personal and professional needs.
- **Technology:** Leveraging technology to stay connected and productive from various locations.
- **Mindset:** Shifting from the notion of "balance" to "integration," understanding that work and life can overlap and coexist.
- **Boundaries:** Setting boundaries to manage work and personal life demands effectively.
- **Well-Being:** Prioritizing mental and physical health by integrating self-care practices into daily routines.

Work-Life Integration emphasizes creating a personalized approach that aligns with individual lifestyles and preferences, fostering a sense of control and satisfaction in both work and personal life.

The Evolution from Work-Life Balance to Work-Life Integration:

The evolution from work-life balance to work-life integration involves shifting from separating work and personal life to blending them seamlessly, allowing for more flexibility and holistic well-being.

Historical Perspective on Work-Life Balance:

It examines the changing dynamics of managing professional and personal life over time, highlighting the shift from balancing separate domains to integrating them seamlessly.

- Work-life balance emerged as a concept in the late 20th century, emphasizing the need to separate work and personal life to prevent burnout and maintain health.
- Initially, it focused on working hours, advocating for fixed working hours and a clear separation between professional and personal time.

Reasons for the Shift Towards Integration:

It includes the growing need for flexibility, technological advancements, and changing societal expectations.

- Technological advancements allow for more flexible working conditions, blurring the lines between work and personal life.
- The rise of remote work and the gig economy, where traditional boundaries are less defined.
- Changing societal values, with more emphasis on holistic well-being and personal fulfillment.

Benefits of Work-Life Integration:

It involves achieving a harmonious blend of professional and personal responsibilities, leading to increased productivity, well-being, and overall life satisfaction.

Improved Mental Health and Well-Being:

Achieving a harmonious balance between work and personal life leads to reduced stress and enhanced overall emotional and psychological health.

- Reduced stress as individuals can manage their responsibilities more flexibly.
- Better work satisfaction and personal fulfillment.
- Increased Productivity and Job Satisfaction:
- Flexibility can lead to more efficient work patterns tailored to individual peak productivity times.
- Higher job satisfaction as employees feel more in control of their schedules.

Better Relationships and Family Time:

Achieving work-life integration fosters stronger family bonds and improves personal relationships by ensuring quality time and emotional presence.

- More opportunities to spend time with family and friends, enhancing personal relationships.
- Ability to be present for significant personal events without compromising work responsibilities.

Challenges of Work-Life Integration:

The challenges of work-life integration involve balancing professional responsibilities and personal life demands without sacrificing performance or well-being in either domain.

- **Difficulty in Setting Boundaries**: Blurred lines can make it hard to switch off from work, leading to potential burnout. The risk of overworking as work is always accessible.
- **Overlap of Work and Personal Time**: Potential conflicts when work demands intrude into personal or family time.

- **Potential for Burnout:** Constant connectivity can lead to fatigue and decreased overall well-being if not managed properly.

Strategies for Effective Work-Life Integration:

Strategies for Effective Work-Life Integration involve balancing professional responsibilities and personal life through prioritization, time management, and setting boundaries to achieve overall well-being.

- **Flexible Work Arrangements:** Implementing flexible working hours and locations. Allowing remote work or hybrid models.
- **Time Management Techniques:** Prioritizing tasks and setting clear goals. Using productivity tools and apps to organize work and personal responsibilities.
- **Use of Technology and Tools:** Leveraging communication and collaboration tools for efficient remote work. Utilizing time-tracking apps to balance work and personal activities.

Role of Employers in Promoting Work-Life Integration:

Employers play a crucial role in promoting work-life integration by implementing policies and practices that support employees in balancing their professional and personal lives.

- **Policies and Programs That Support Integration:** Introducing policies like flexible working hours, remote work options, and family leave. Providing resources for mental health and well-being.
- **Creating a Supportive Workplace Culture:** Encouraging a culture that values personal time and well-being. Promoting open communication about work-life needs.
- **Training and Development Opportunities:** Offering training programs that help employees manage work and personal life better. Providing career development opportunities that align with personal goals.

Technology and Work-Life Integration:

Technology and Work-Life Integration refers to the use of digital tools and platforms to harmonize professional responsibilities with personal life, enhancing flexibility and productivity.

- **Role of Remote Work Tools:** Tools like Zoom, Slack, and Microsoft Teams facilitate remote collaboration.
- **Digital Communication and Collaboration Platforms:** Platforms that allow asynchronous communication to accommodate different time zones and schedules.
- **Managing Digital Distractions:** Strategies for minimizing distractions, such as setting specific work hours and using focus modes on devices.

Work-Life Integration for Different Demographics:

It refers to the harmonious blending of professional and personal responsibilities tailored to the unique needs and circumstances of various population groups.

- **Approaches for Working Parents:** Flexible schedules to accommodate childcare needs. Policies for parental leave and childcare support.
- **Strategies for Single Professionals:** Encouraging social activities and personal development opportunities. Balancing work and personal growth.
- **Considerations for Remote Workers:** Addressing isolation by fostering a virtual community and regular check-ins. Providing resources for home office setups.

Future Trends in Work-Life Integration:

Future Trends in Work-Life Integration focus on blending professional and personal life seamlessly, leveraging technology and flexible work environments to enhance productivity and well-being.

- **Impact of the Gig Economy and Freelance Work:** The rise of freelancing and gig work and its effect on traditional work structures.
- **Predictions for Post-Pandemic Work Environments:** How the COVID-19 pandemic has accelerated remote work adoption and what the future holds.
- **Emerging Technologies and Their Potential Effects:** The role of AI, VR, and other technologies in shaping the future of work-life integration.

Work-Life Integration and Mental Health:

Work-Life Integration and Mental Health refers to the seamless blend of personal and professional responsibilities to promote overall well-being and mental health.

- **Stress Management Techniques:** Practices like mindfulness, meditation, and exercise to manage stress.
- **Importance of Self-Care:** Incorporating self-care routines into daily life for better mental health.
- **Resources and Support Systems:** Access to mental health resources, employee assistance programs, and support groups.

Cultural Differences in Work-Life Integration:

Cultural Differences in Work-Life Integration refers to the varying ways different societies balance professional responsibilities and personal life, influenced by cultural values, norms, and expectations.

- **Comparison of Practices in Different Countries:** How different cultures approach work-life integration, such as Scandinavian countries' emphasis on work-life balance versus the work-centric culture in countries like Japan.
- **Influence of Cultural Values on Work-Life Integration Approaches:** How cultural values shape policies and practices around work and personal life integration.

Measuring Success in Work-Life Integration:

It involves assessing the balance and satisfaction between professional responsibilities and personal life commitments.

- **Metrics and Indicators of Successful Integration:** Identifying key indicators such as employee satisfaction, productivity levels, and turnover rates.
- **Tools and Methods for Assessment:** Surveys, feedback mechanisms, and performance evaluations to measure the effectiveness of work-life integration efforts.

> *"It is not advisable to consistently prioritize work over family or vice versa. Instead, strive for a balanced work-life integration that enables you to allocate time effectively between both work and family, ensuring you can fully appreciate and enjoy all aspects of life."*

Companies with Successful Work-Life Integration Policies:

Successful work-life integration policies are increasingly valued by employees and crucial for companies aiming to attract and retain talent. Here are key aspects often found in companies with successful work-life integration policies:

- **Flexible Work Arrangements:** Companies offer options like flextime, telecommuting, or compressed workweeks to accommodate personal schedules and reduce commuting stress.
- **Generous Parental Leave:** Providing substantial parental leave, beyond legal requirements, supports employees during significant life events without compromising their career progression.
- **Support for Caregivers:** Policies that assist employees caring for elderly parents or family members, such as caregiving leave or access to resources, demonstrate understanding and support.
- **Wellness Programs:** Initiatives promoting physical and mental well-being, like onsite fitness facilities, wellness days, or counseling services, contribute to a healthier work-life balance.

- **Technology Use:** Leveraging technology to facilitate remote work, enhance communication, and enable flexibility in work locations helps employees manage responsibilities more effectively.
- **Clear Communication and Expectations:** Transparent communication about workload expectations, deadlines, and performance metrics helps employees plan and prioritize effectively.
- **Employee Support Initiatives:** Employee assistance programs (EAPs), financial planning support, or workshops on stress management and work-life balance foster a supportive environment.
- **Culture of Trust and Respect:** Cultivating a workplace culture that values results over presenteeism, respects personal boundaries, and encourages work-life balance as a norm.
- **Leadership Example:** Senior leaders demonstrating and advocating for work-life balance encourages its adoption across all levels of the organization.
- **Feedback Mechanisms:** Regular feedback loops where employees can suggest improvements or voice concerns about work-life balance policies ensure continuous refinement and relevance.

Companies that successfully implement these policies not only improve employee satisfaction and retention but also enhance productivity and innovation by fostering a healthier, more engaged workforce.

> *"In any company, it's crucial for seniors to communicate politely with juniors, offer help generously, and teach everything calmly. This fosters a bond of respect that should persist even if employees change companies. This mutual respect forms the foundation for a successful company culture."*

Finding Harmony: A Story of Work-Life Integration:

Characters:

- **Sarah Miller:** *A marketing manager at a tech company.*
- **John Miller:** *Sarah's husband, a freelance graphic designer.*
- **Emily:** *Their 6-year-old daughter.*
- **Max:** *Their Labrador Retriever.*

Sarah Miller sat in her home office, a sunlit corner of her living room, sipping her morning coffee as she reviewed her to-do list. It was 8:30 AM, and she had an important video call with her team at 9. John, her husband, was in the kitchen packing Emily's lunch for school. Max, their playful Labrador, lounged at Sarah's feet, occasionally nudging her for a pat.

Three years ago, Sarah's life was a constant juggling act. She commuted over an hour each way to her office, often missing family dinners and bedtime stories with Emily. John's freelance work gave him more flexibility, but they struggled to sync their schedules. Weekends were filled with catch-up work, leaving little time for relaxation or family activities.

The shift began when Sarah's company introduced a flexible work policy. Remote work became the norm, allowing employees to manage their schedules more freely. At first, Sarah was skeptical. How would she maintain her productivity amidst household distractions?

But as weeks turned into months, Sarah discovered the beauty of work-life integration.

Morning Routine:*Sarah's mornings started with family breakfast. Instead of rushing out the door, she enjoyed her coffee while chatting with John and Emily. After dropping Emily at school, she walked Max around the neighborhood, using the time to clear her mind and plan her day.*

Work Hours:*By 9 AM, Sarah was at her desk, joining the team call. The tech company had adopted various collaboration tools, making remote communication seamless. Sarah found herself more productive without the constant interruptions of office life. She scheduled deep work periods in the morning, tackling complex projects when her mind was sharpest.*

John, working from his home studio, had his routine. They coordinated their schedules, ensuring one was always available for Emily. They shared a Google Calendar to keep track of work commitments, school activities, and family time.

Afternoon Breaks:*At noon, Sarah took a break. She and John often had lunch together, a simple yet significant change that strengthened their relationship. Some days, she used the time to attend a yoga class or run errands. The flexibility allowed her to weave personal tasks into her workday, reducing the mental load of a long to-do list.*

Family Time:*By 3 PM, it was time to pick up Emily. Sarah scheduled her meetings and work tasks around this, often finishing her work later in the evening if needed. The afternoons were dedicated to family. They helped Emily with her homework, took Max to the park, or enjoyed a quiet afternoon together.*

Evening Routine:*Post-dinner, Sarah sometimes logged back on to finish her work, but without the stress of a ticking clock. John often did the same, finding inspiration in the quiet hours. They had clear boundaries, ensuring work didn't creep into their time excessively.*

Weekends:*Weekends transformed from catch-up work sessions to family adventures. They took short trips, explored new hobbies, and had movie nights. The balance they achieved made their time together more meaningful.*

Conclusion:*Over time, Sarah realized that work-life integration wasn't about blending work and personal life into a chaotic mix. It was about creating a harmonious rhythm that allowed both to coexist peacefully. She felt more in control, less stressed, and more fulfilled as a professional and a mother.*

Sarah's journey wasn't without challenges. There were days when work demands were high, and personal responsibilities felt overwhelming. But with open communication, flexibility, and a supportive work environment, she navigated these hurdles.

Looking back, Sarah couldn't imagine returning to her old routine. Work-life integration had given her a new perspective on what it meant to live a balanced, fulfilling life. And as she looked around at her happy family, she knew it was worth every step of the journey.

"Work-life integration is not about balance; it's about making sure that your work and personal life are in harmony with each other. - **Satyam Tyagi***"*

11

Mastering Money

Money management is a vital skill for building a secure future. We offer practical tips on budgeting, saving, and investing wisely, empowering you to take control of your financial destiny.

Mastering Money refers to gaining control over your financial situation through effective management, planning, and strategies. It involves understanding and implementing key financial principles to achieve financial stability and growth. Here are some key aspects:

Budgeting:

Budgeting is a fundamental skill in mastering money management. It involves creating a plan for how to allocate your income and expenses over a certain period.

Creating a Budget:

Budgeting is the process of creating a detailed plan that outlines where and how you will spend your money. This plan is called a budget, and it helps you ensure that you are living within your means and working towards your financial goals.

- **Income Tracking:** List all sources of income, including salary, freelance work, and passive income.
- **Expense Tracking:** Categorize and track all expenses, from fixed costs like rent and utilities to variable costs like groceries and entertainment.
- **Budgeting Tools:** Use tools like spreadsheets, apps, or traditional pen and paper to create and manage your budget.

Expense Management:

Expense Management is a crucial aspect of mastering money. It involves tracking, analyzing, and controlling how money is spent within an organization or personal finance system.

- **Needs vs. Wants:** Differentiate between essential expenses (needs) and discretionary spending (wants).
- **Cutting Costs:** Identify areas where you can reduce spending, such as dining out, subscription services, or impulse purchases.

Savings:

Savings in the context of mastering money refers to the practice of setting aside a portion of one's income or earnings for future use, rather than spending it immediately. It is a fundamental aspect of personal finance and financial planning.

Emergency Fund:

An Emergency Fund is a financial safety net designed to cover unexpected expenses or financial emergencies, such as medical bills, car repairs, or sudden loss of income.

- **Fund Size:** Aim to save 3-6 months' worth of living expenses to cover unexpected costs like medical emergencies, car repairs, or job loss.
- **Access:** Keep the fund in a high-yield savings account for easy access.

Short-Term and Long-Term Savings:

Short-Term and Long-Term Savings are key concepts in personal finance, essential for mastering money management. Understanding these concepts helps individuals plan for immediate needs and future goals.

- **Short-term Goals:** Save for goals within the next 1-5 years, such as vacations, a new car, or home renovations.
- **Long-term Goals:** Save for future needs beyond 5 years, like a child's education or retirement, by contributing regularly to savings or investment accounts.

Investing:

Investing is a fundamental aspect of mastering money, and it involves allocating resources, usually in the form of capital, with the expectation of generating income or profit over time.

Investment Options:

Investment Options refer to the various avenues through which individuals can allocate their money to generate returns over time. Mastering money involves understanding these options and making informed choices to grow one's wealth.

- **Stocks:** Ownership shares in companies that can provide dividends and capital appreciation.
- **Bonds:** Debt securities that pay interest over a fixed period are considered safer than stocks.
- **Mutual Funds:** Pooled funds managed by professionals that invest in a diversified portfolio of stocks, bonds, or other assets.
- **Real Estate:** Property investments that can provide rental income and appreciate over time.

Risk Management:

Risk Management in the context of mastering money refers to identifying, assessing, and prioritizing risks followed by coordinated efforts to minimize, monitor, and control the impact of unfortunate events on one's financial situation. It involves a range of strategies and tools designed to help individuals protect their assets, achieve financial goals, and ensure long-term financial stability.

- **Diversification:** Spread investments across different asset classes and sectors to reduce risk.
- **Asset Allocation:** Adjust the mix of investments based on risk tolerance, financial goals, and time horizon.

Debt Management:

Debt Management is a crucial aspect of mastering money and involves strategies and practices to handle and repay debt effectively.

Debt Reduction:

Debt Reduction is a key concept in mastering money, focusing on decreasing the total amount of debt you owe to improve your financial health.

- **High-Interest Debts:** Focus on paying off high-interest debts like credit card balances first to reduce interest costs.
- **Debt Repayment Strategies:** Use methods like the debt snowball (paying off smallest debts first) or debt avalanche (paying off highest interest debts first).

Credit Management:

Credit Management refers to the practices and strategies individuals or businesses use to manage their credit responsibly. It involves understanding and effectively utilizing credit facilities such as loans, credit cards, or lines of credit while maintaining a good credit score and managing debt levels sensibly.

- **Credit Score:** Maintain a good credit score by paying bills on time, reducing debt, and avoiding unnecessary credit inquiries.
- **Credit Utilization:** Keep credit card balances low relative to credit limits.

Financial Planning:

Financial Planning refers to the process of managing your money to achieve specific financial goals and objectives. It involves assessing your current financial situation, setting goals, and creating a plan to achieve them.

Setting Financial Goals:

Setting Financial Goals is a crucial aspect of mastering money and personal finance. It involves defining specific objectives that you want to achieve with your finances over a certain period.

- **SMART Goals:** Set Specific, Measurable, Achievable, Relevant, and Time-bound financial goals.
- **Goal Prioritization:** Rank goals by importance and timeframe, focusing on immediate priorities first.

Retirement Planning:

Retirement Planning in the context of mastering money refers to the strategic process of setting financial goals and creating a plan to achieve financial independence and security during retirement years.

- **Retirement Accounts:** Contribute to tax-advantaged retirement accounts like 401(k)s, IRAs, or Roth IRAs.
- **Employer Matching:** Take full advantage of employer-matching contributions in retirement plans.

Income Generation:

Income Generation refers to the process of earning money through various means. It encompasses activities and strategies that individuals or businesses undertake to generate revenue and increase their financial resources.

Multiple Income Streams:

"Multiple Income Streams" refers to the strategy of generating income from various sources rather than relying solely on one source, such as a job salary.

- **Side Hustles:** Explore part-time jobs, freelance work, or gig economy opportunities to supplement income.
- **Passive Income:** Invest in rental properties, dividend-paying stocks, or create digital products that generate ongoing income.

Career Development:

Career Development in the context of mastering money refers to the process of advancing one's professional growth and achieving financial stability through strategic career choices and actions.

- **Skill Enhancement:** Continuously develop skills through courses, certifications, and training.
- **Networking:** Build a professional network to discover new opportunities and advance your career.

Financial Education:

Financial Education refers to the process of learning and understanding how money works, including managing, investing, saving, and spending it wisely. It involves acquiring knowledge and skills that empower individuals to make informed and effective financial decisions throughout their lives.

Continuous Learning:

Continuous Learning in the context of mastering money refers to the ongoing process of acquiring knowledge and skills related to financial management, investing, and personal finance.

- **Reading and Research:** Stay informed by reading books, articles, and financial news.
- **Financial Literacy Courses:** Enroll in online or in-person courses to deepen your financial knowledge.

Seeking Professional Advice:

Seeking Professional Advice in mastering money refers to the practice of consulting with financial experts or professionals to make informed decisions about managing finances and investments. This advice typically comes from financial planners, investment advisors, or wealth managers who have expertise in areas such as budgeting, saving, investing, tax planning, retirement planning, and wealth preservation.

- **Financial Advisors:** Consult with certified financial planners or advisors for personalized financial planning and investment advice.
- **Tax Professionals:** Work with accountants or tax professionals to optimize tax strategies.

Mindset and Habits:

Mindset and Habits in mastering money refer to the foundational beliefs and behaviors that influence how individuals manage and grow their finances effectively.

Financial Discipline:

Financial Discipline refers to the practice of managing your finances in a responsible and organized manner.

- **Regular Saving:** Automate savings by setting up automatic transfers to savings accounts.
- **Wise Spending:** Practice mindful spending by evaluating purchases and avoiding impulse buys.

Positive Money Mindset:

Positive Money Mindset refers to the attitudes, beliefs, and perspectives one holds about money that contribute to effective financial management and wealth building.

- **Healthy Attitude:** Cultivate a positive relationship with money by focusing on financial goals and celebrating progress.
- **Wealth-Building:** Embrace a growth mindset that sees financial challenges as opportunities for learning and improvement.

Mastering money involves a comprehensive approach that combines practical strategies, continuous education, and a disciplined mindset to achieve financial stability, growth, and overall well-being.

> *"I'm not saying you should spend all your salary on savings, nor am I saying you should spend it all on household expenses. What I'm suggesting is that you allocate 50% of your money to savings, 30% to household expenses, and the remaining 20% for leisure activities like dining out, parties, or whatever else you enjoy in your free time."*

The Path to Financial Mastery: A Real-World Tale

Characters:

- **Ravi Mehta:***An IT professional in his late 20s.*
- **Priya Mehta:***Ravi's wife, a school teacher.*
- **Sanjay:***Ravi's old college friend and financial planner.*

Ravi Mehta sat at his kitchen table, staring at a pile of bills and a dwindling bank balance. Despite working a stable job in IT and his wife Priya working as a teacher, they struggled to save and often found themselves living paycheck to paycheck. The stress of financial instability was starting to take a toll on their relationship.

The Realization: *One weekend, Ravi ran into his old college friend, Sanjay, at a reunion. Sanjay, now a financial planner, listened as Ravi vented about his financial struggles. "You need a plan, Ravi," Sanjay said. "Money management isn't just about earning more; it's about mastering the money you have."*

The First Step - Budgeting: *Sanjay offered to help Ravi and Priya get their finances in order. The first step was creating a budget. Sanjay helped them track their income and expenses over a month. They were shocked to see how much they spent on dining out, streaming subscriptions, and impulsive online shopping. They created a budget that prioritized essential expenses and allocated a portion of their income to savings and debt repayment.*

Emergency Fund: *Sanjay emphasized the importance of an emergency fund. Ravi and Priya decided to start small, aiming to save $1,000 initially and then gradually build it up to cover three months of living expenses. They set up an automatic transfer to a high-yield savings account to ensure consistency.*

Tackling Debt: *Next, they focused on their debt. Ravi had a credit card balance with a high interest rate, and Priya had a small student loan. Sanjay recommended the debt avalanche method, prioritizing the high-interest credit card debt while making minimum payments on the student loan. Every extra dollar they saved went towards reducing their debt faster.*

Smart Spending and Saving: *Ravi and Priya started practicing mindful spending. They cooked at home more often, canceled unnecessary subscriptions, and shopped with a list to avoid impulse buys. They also opened a joint savings account for short-term goals like vacations and home improvements.*

Investing for the Future: *With their debt under control and an emergency fund in place, Ravi and Priya turned their attention to investing. Sanjay helped them open a brokerage account and taught them the basics of investing in mutual funds and ETFs. Ravi also started contributing to his employer's 401(k) plan, taking full advantage of the company match.*

Increasing Income: *To boost their savings, Ravi took on freelance IT projects, and Priya offered tutoring services. This additional income allowed them to save more and invest in their future. They also began exploring passive income opportunities, such as renting out their spare room on Airbnb.*

Continuous Learning: *Ravi and Priya made financial education a priority. They read books, attended webinars, and followed personal finance blogs. They scheduled regular check-ins with Sanjay to review their progress and adjust their financial plan as needed.*

Maintaining a Positive Money Mindset: *One of the most significant changes was their mindset. They celebrated small financial victories, like paying off a credit card or reaching a savings milestone. They focused on their long-term goals and remained patient and disciplined.*

Achieving Financial Stability: *Over time, Ravi and Priya saw significant improvements. They paid off all their debts, built a solid emergency fund, and accumulated a growing investment portfolio. They felt more secure and less stressed, enjoying their lives without constant financial worries.*

Epilogue: *Sharing Their Success Inspired by their journey, Ravi and Priya started a community financial education group, sharing their story and tips with friends and neighbors. They organized workshops and online sessions, helping others achieve financial stability and independence.*

Ravi and Priya's story illustrates that mastering money is not about quick fixes or drastic changes. It's about taking consistent, informed steps toward managing finances, setting realistic goals, and continuously learning and adapting. Their journey from financial stress to stability is a testament to the power of discipline, planning, and a positive mindset.

From Financial Struggle to Dream Home: A Journey in Mastering Money:

Facing Financial Challenges: *In a village, Ajay, a 35-year-old salesman, his wife Mahi, and their daughter Lavina struggle with their expenses. Despite Lavina's ongoing educational needs, they found themselves living paycheck to paycheck without any savings for the future.*

The Decision to Invest: *Ajay proposed buying a plot of land outside the village to Mahi, envisioning it as a long-term investment. Mahi initially hesitated, concerned about their ability to afford it alongside their current expenses. Ajay devised a plan to take a loan from the neighbor with interest for the plot, committing to saving a portion of his salary and working overtime to meet their financial goals.*

Investing in Growth: *After careful planning and saving, Ajay and Mahi purchased a plot in a developing area of a nearby city at an affordable price.*

Seizing Opportunities: *As the value of their initial plot increased over time, Ajay sold it and reinvested the profit into a plot in a prime location within the city.*

Financial Discipline: *Ajay and Mahi diligently paid off their loans in installments, managing their expenses and prioritizing savings. Lavina also secured a job, further stabilizing their financial situation.*

Building Their Dream Home: *Confident in their financial stability, Ajay and Mahi decided to move from the village to the city. They secured another loan to build a home on their plot, fulfilling their dream of a comfortable and secure living space.*

Achieving Financial Freedom: *Through careful expense management, consistent overtime work, and strategic investments, Ajay and Mahi paid off their loans and established a happy and fulfilling life in their unexpected dream home.*

Epilogue: *The Power of Money Mastery Ajay and Mahi's journey demonstrates how mastering money involves foresight, perseverance, and wise decision-making. By taking calculated risks and maintaining financial discipline, they transformed financial challenges into opportunities and achieved their dreams.*

"*Beware of little expenses. A small leak will sink a great ship. -* **Benjamin Franklin**"

12
Lifestyle Choices and Cultural Identity

Lifestyle choices and cultural identity are deeply interconnected. Lifestyle encompasses how people live, including their habits, attitudes, and values. Cultural identity refers to belonging to a particular culture or group. The interplay between these two concepts influences how individuals express themselves and how societies function.

Lifestyle Choices:

Lifestyle Choices refers to the decisions and habits individuals make regarding their daily activities, health, and overall way of living, which collectively shape their quality of life and well-being.

- **Diet and Food Preferences:** Dietary habits are often influenced by cultural traditions. For example, Mediterranean diets are rich in fruits, vegetables, and olive oil, reflecting the agricultural practices and health philosophies of that region.

  "The foundation of the Mediterranean diet is plant foods. That means meals are built around vegetables, fruits, herbs, nuts, beans and whole grains. Moderate amounts of dairy, poultry and eggs are part of the Mediterranean diet, as is seafood."

- **Clothing and Fashion:** Traditional attire and modern fashion choices can reflect cultural heritage and identity. For instance, wearing a kimono in Japan or a sari in India can signify a connection to cultural roots.
- **Social Behaviors and Etiquette:** Norms around greetings, hospitality, and social interactions vary widely. For example, bowing in Japan versus shaking hands in Western cultures or greeting in India.
- **Leisure Activities and Hobbies:** Choices in entertainment and hobbies can be culturally driven. The popularity of cricket in India and Latin America versus American football in the United States highlights cultural preferences.

How Lifestyles Should Be Shaped:

In today's fast-paced world, finding a meaningful and balanced lifestyle is crucial. A fulfilling life isn't just about success and achievements; it's about health, relationships, growth, and inner peace.

Healthy Living:

- **Balanced Diet:** Imagine a mother preparing a nutritious meal for her children, ensuring they grow up strong and healthy. A balanced diet isn't just about eating right; it's about caring for our bodies and those we love.
- **Regular Exercise:** Picture an elderly man walking in the park every morning, finding joy and strength in each step. Regular exercise is about more than fitness; it's about living life to the fullest, no matter our age.
- **Adequate Sleep:** Think of a young student, finally getting a good night's sleep after days of studying. Quality sleep restores our energy and renews our spirit, enabling us to face each day with vitality.

Positive Relationships:

- **Family and Friends:** Envision a family gathered around the dinner table, sharing stories and laughter. Strong relationships with family and friends are the bedrock of a happy life, providing support and love in every moment.
- **Community Engagement:** Imagine a community coming together to help a neighbor in need. Engaging with our community gives us a sense of belonging and purpose, reminding us that we are never alone.

Personal Growth:

- **Continuous Learning:** Picture an adult returning to school, driven by a passion for knowledge and self-improvement. Lifelong learning opens doors and keeps our minds alive, fueling our dreams and aspirations.
- **Self-Care:** Think of someone taking time to meditate, paint, or simply relax in a peaceful setting. Self-care is about nurturing our soul, finding joy in the simple pleasures, and reconnecting with ourselves.

Balance and Mindfulness:

- **Work-Life Balance:** Imagine a parent leaving work early to attend their child's school play. Striking a balance between work and personal life allows us to cherish the moments that truly matter.
- **Mindfulness and Stress Management:** Picture someone practicing yoga at sunrise, finding tranquility amid chaos. Mindfulness helps us stay grounded and resilient, facing life's challenges with a calm and clear mind.

An ideal lifestyle is about more than just physical health and success. It's about the small moments of joy, the connections we build, and the peace we find within ourselves. By embracing a balanced and mindful approach to life, we can create a more meaningful and heartwarming existence for ourselves and those around us.

"We have often heard people telling each other that they haven't truly enjoyed life, labeling their experiences as boring. Ironically, 90% of those who say this consider having fast food at street vendors as "enjoying life." They spend a little money on fast food and then boast to their friends, claiming they're living life to the fullest while mocking others who don't join in. And they aren't joking—they're quite serious in these discussions.

If someone happens to be a bit introverted, speaks less, doesn't drink, avoids movies, malls, or travel, they're often seen as part of the 20% who are different. Meanwhile, the other 80% proudly declare themselves as the ones truly living life. Neither group is wrong; they just have different ways of experiencing life. Yet, the 80% frequently insult the 20%, saying their lifestyle is poor and calling them a burden on the earth.

Some people drink excessively, causing disturbances when they return home, and even resorting to violence against their children and spouse because of alcohol. Alcohol consumption should be limited to occasional instances, and only if one truly desires to drink, not because of peer pressure. Some individuals know their limits and manage to maintain a healthy lifestyle even after drinking. Thus, moderation is essential, whether it's related to alcohol, exercise, diet, or academics.

People should incorporate into their lifestyle a readiness to help others, whether by providing education, financial assistance, emotional support, or aid with health issues."

Cultural Identity:

Cultural identity refers to the sense of belonging and identification with a particular cultural group or heritage

- **Language:** Language is a core component of cultural identity. It shapes communication and can influence worldview. Multilingual individuals often navigate multiple cultural identities.
- **Religion and Spirituality:** Religious beliefs and practices are significant in shaping cultural identity. They influence moral values, rituals, and community structures.
- **Traditions and Customs:** Celebrations, festivals, and rituals play a key role in maintaining cultural identity. Examples include Diwali in India, Thanksgiving in the United States, and the Dragon Boat Festival in China.
- **Shared History and Ancestry:** Historical events and ancestry contribute to a sense of belonging. Narratives of past struggles, achievements, and migrations are central to cultural identity.

Interplay Between Lifestyle Choices and Cultural Identity:

The interplay between lifestyle choices and cultural identity explores how personal preferences and behaviors intersect with and reflect one's cultural heritage and values.

- **Adaptation and Change:** Globalization and migration lead to the blending of cultures. People may adopt new lifestyle choices while retaining elements of their cultural identity, creating hybrid cultures.
- **Resistance and Preservation:** Some communities actively resist cultural assimilation to preserve their unique identity. This can be seen in the revival of indigenous languages and traditions.
- **Cultural Pride and Expression:** Lifestyle choices can be a form of expressing cultural pride. For example, African Americans celebrate Juneteenth or wear Afrocentric clothing to honor their heritage.
- **Identity Conflicts and Negotiation:** Individuals navigating multiple cultural identities may face conflicts. Bicultural or multicultural individuals often negotiate between different sets of cultural norms and expectations.

Understanding the relationship between lifestyle choices and cultural identity is crucial for appreciating the diversity of human experience. It highlights how individuals and communities shape and are shaped by their cultural contexts. The dynamic interplay between these elements fosters a rich tapestry of global cultures.

The Tale of Ravi and Priya: Lifestyle Choices & Cultural Identity

In the vibrant city of Jaipur, two childhood friends, Ravi and Priya, grew up with contrasting lifestyles that shaped their paths in unique ways. Their story reflects the impact of lifestyle choices on personal growth and cultural identity.

Ravi's Path - Embracing Tradition: Ravi belonged to a traditional Rajasthani family that deeply valued their cultural heritage. His parents, both school teachers, instilled in him the importance of following customs and maintaining a connection to their roots. Ravi's lifestyle was a blend of modern education and traditional practices.

Family and Community: Ravi spent weekends attending community events, where he learned folk dances and played traditional instruments. His evenings were filled with storytelling sessions with his grandparents, where he absorbed the wisdom of ancient tales.

Diet and Health: Ravi's family adhered to a diet rich in local produce, homemade ghee, and traditional spices. They believed in the healing power of Ayurveda, and Ravi often accompanied his grandmother to the local markets to buy fresh herbs and vegetables.

Education and Career: While Ravi pursued engineering, he remained connected to his cultural roots. He participated in college cultural festivals, performing folk dances and organizing events that showcased Rajasthani heritage. After graduation, he joined a company that valued cultural preservation, working on projects that promoted sustainable tourism in Rajasthan.

Priya's Journey - Embracing Modernity: Priya, on the other hand, was born to a progressive family that encouraged her to explore the world beyond traditional boundaries. Her parents, both doctors, believed in balancing cultural values with a modern outlook. Priya's lifestyle was a blend of innovation and cultural appreciation.

Exploring New Horizons: Priya was an avid traveler, and her family's vacations often took them to different parts of India and abroad. These trips broadened her perspective and introduced her to diverse cultures and lifestyles.

Health and Fitness: Priya was passionate about fitness and healthy living. She experimented with different cuisines, incorporating global superfoods into her diet. Her mornings began with yoga, followed by jogging in the nearby park.

Education and Career: Priya pursued a degree in fashion design, drawing inspiration from various cultures. Her designs were a fusion of traditional Indian textiles and contemporary styles. After college, she started her fashion label, promoting sustainable fashion and empowering local artisans.

Intersections and Reflections: Despite their different paths, Ravi and Priya remained close friends. They often reflected on their lifestyles and the choices they made. Ravi admired Priya's adventurous spirit and modern outlook, while Priya respected Ravi's deep connection to his roots.

Learning from Each Other: Ravi began to incorporate some of Priya's fitness routines into his life, realizing the importance of physical health. Priya, in turn, embraced some traditional practices, like Ayurveda, and began attending community events with Ravi.

Balancing Tradition and Modernity: Together, they discovered the beauty of balancing tradition with modernity. They organized cultural events that showcased traditional arts in contemporary settings, blending their passions and creating something unique.

Conclusion:

Ravi and Priya's story illustrates that lifestyle choices are deeply personal and influenced by a myriad of factors, including family, culture, and personal aspirations. Their journey shows that whether one embraces tradition or modernity, or a blend of both, what matters most is finding fulfillment and staying true to oneself. In the end, it's the respect and understanding of each other's choices that enrich our lives and strengthen our cultural identity.

"Cultural identity is not something that is given to you; it is something that you build over time through your lifestyle choices and experiences. - **Satyam Tyagi***"*

13
Every Story Matters

"Every Story Matters" emphasizes the significance of each individual's experiences and perspectives in shaping the broader human narrative. This concept asserts that every person's story, regardless of its scope or scale, holds value and contributes to the diversity and richness of our collective existence.

Recognizing that "Every Story Matters" encourages empathy, inclusivity, and respect. It invites us to listen to and appreciate the varied life experiences of others, fostering a deeper understanding and connection between people. By valuing each story, we acknowledge the unique challenges, triumphs, and lessons that everyone brings to the table, creating a more compassionate and integrated society where every voice is heard and honored.

Furthermore, "Every Story Matters" highlights the idea that no story is too small or insignificant to make an impact. Each person's journey is filled with moments of growth, resilience, and wisdom that can inspire and teach others. Whether it is a story of overcoming adversity, achieving personal goals, or simply navigating everyday life, these narratives contribute to a mosaic of human experience that is both complex and beautiful.

In a world where it is easy to feel overlooked or unheard, embracing the belief that "Every Story Matters" empowers individuals to share their truths and be confident in the value of their experiences. It also reminds us to approach others with an open heart and mind, recognizing that we all have unique stories that deserve to be acknowledged and celebrated.

By creating spaces—whether in our communities, workplaces, or social circles—where stories can be shared and valued, we foster an environment of mutual respect and understanding. This not only strengthens bond between people but also promotes a culture of empathy and support that benefits everyone.

In essence, "Every Story Matters" is a call to honor the individuality and humanity of each person, acknowledging that our collective narrative is richer and more meaningful when we embrace the diverse tapestry of stories that make up our world.

The Invisible Men: Recognizing Average Students' Stories:

In a typical classroom, attention often gravitates toward the brilliant students who consistently excel and the backbenchers who struggle and require additional support. However, nestled between these two extremes are the average students, whose voices and stories frequently go unnoticed. These students have unique stories filled with challenges, strengths, and aspirations. By acknowledging that "Every Story Matters," educators can create an inclusive environment where every student feels valued. Recognizing the experiences of average students enriches education for everyone, ensuring all voices are heard and contributions appreciated. This fosters a culture of empathy, support, and holistic development in the classroom.

Take Raj, for instance. Raj was neither at the top of his class nor at the bottom. He consistently achieved average grades and was seldom called upon by teachers. Despite his quiet demeanor, Raj had a story filled with determination and resilience. He balanced his studies with helping out at his family's small shop, spending long hours after school assisting his parents to make ends meet.

Raj's experiences taught him valuable lessons in responsibility, time management, and empathy. He was a dependable friend, always ready to lend a helping hand, and had a knack for solving practical problems. Yet, his contributions often went unrecognized in the classroom.

Similarly, Priya, another average student, loved literature and wrote beautiful poems in her free time. She dreamt of becoming a writer one day but rarely had the opportunity to share her passion in a classroom that focused primarily on measurable academic achievements. Her creative spirit and unique perspective added richness to her understanding of the world, but they remained hidden under the label of "average."

Recognizing that "Every Story Matters" means acknowledging the unique journeys of students like Raj and Priya. It involves teachers taking the time to understand the individual strengths, challenges, and aspirations of each student, beyond their grades. By creating an inclusive learning environment, educators can ensure that every student feels seen, heard, and valued.

This approach encourages teachers to adopt diverse teaching methods that cater to different learning styles and to provide opportunities for all students to shine in various aspects, whether it's through creative projects, group discussions, or practical applications of knowledge. It also involves fostering a classroom culture where students support and learn from each other, recognizing that everyone has something valuable to contribute.

Ultimately, valuing the stories of average students enriches the educational experience for everyone, promoting a sense of belonging and encouraging all students to pursue their passions and potential. It reminds us that every student, regardless of where they fall on the academic spectrum, has a unique story that deserves recognition and appreciation.

Importance of Focusing on Average Students:

It refers to the recognition of the need to provide additional support and resources to students who perform at an average level, ensuring they receive the attention and guidance necessary to reach their full potential and succeed academically.

- **Personal Growth and Potential**: Average students often possess untapped potential that goes unnoticed. For instance, consider Anjali, who consistently scores average grades in her subjects. However, Anjali has a keen interest in environmental science and often participates in local clean-up drives. By recognizing and nurturing her passion, educators can help Anjali discover her strengths and grow beyond her perceived limitations.
- **Balanced Classroom Dynamics:** A balanced focus on all students creates a more equitable and dynamic classroom environment. For example, teachers can incorporate peer-to-peer learning activities where average students like Ravi, who excels in group projects but struggles with exams, can demonstrate leadership and collaboration skills, contributing to a richer learning experience for everyone.
- **Holistic Development:** Education is not just about academic achievement but also about personal and social development. Consider Sara, an average student who is a compassionate listener and a mediator among her peers. By acknowledging her emotional intelligence and

encouraging her to take on roles that require these skills, teachers can promote holistic development and ensure every student's unique abilities are recognized.

- **Encouraging Self-Confidence:** Average students often face issues with self-confidence due to a lack of recognition. Imagine Daniel, who feels overshadowed by his high-achieving classmates. When teachers provide positive reinforcement and opportunities for Daniel to showcase his talents in art and music, it boosts his self-esteem and motivates him to excel in other areas as well.
- **Diverse Learning Styles:** Every student has a unique learning style. Average students like Emma might not excel in traditional exams but show remarkable understanding in hands-on projects. By diversifying teaching methods and assessment strategies, educators can cater to different learning styles, ensuring that students like Emma can thrive and feel valued for their unique approaches to learning.
- **Future Success and Happiness:** The focus on only top achievers can create undue pressure and neglect the overall well-being of students. Average students like John, who have a balanced approach to academics and extracurricular activities, often grow up to lead fulfilling lives with successful careers and healthy relationships. Recognizing and supporting their balanced development is crucial for their long-term happiness and success.

By incorporating these contexts into their teaching strategies, educators can ensure that average students receive the attention and support they deserve, fostering a more inclusive and supportive learning environment.

The Rise of an Average Student:

In a small town, there lived a boy named Arjun. Throughout his school years, Arjun was always an average student. He scored decently on tests, participated in extracurricular activities, and had a group of supportive friends. However, he was often overshadowed by the top achievers and the students who needed extra help. Teachers and classmates alike seldom noticed him, and he quietly went about his studies without much recognition.

Despite this, Arjun had a deep-seated passion for technology. He spent hours at home tinkering with old gadgets, learning programming from online tutorials, and dreaming of creating something impactful. His parents, though supportive, were worried about his future, given his average academic record.

After finishing school, Arjun enrolled in a local college, choosing a course in computer science. Here, he met Professor Mehta, who saw beyond his grades and recognized his genuine interest and potential in technology. Professor Mehta encouraged Arjun to pursue his passion, guiding him on various projects and introducing him to the world of tech startups.

Arjun's dedication paid off when he developed an innovative app designed to help farmers optimize their irrigation systems. This app, initially a college project, gained significant attention for its practical application and potential impact on agriculture. With Professor Mehta's encouragement, Arjun entered his app in a national competition, where he won first place.

This achievement opened doors for Arjun. He received funding and mentorship from leading tech entrepreneurs and was able to refine and expand his app. Eventually, Arjun founded his own startup, which became a critical tool for farmers across the country, significantly improving their productivity and livelihoods.

Arjun's journey from an unnoticed average student to a successful entrepreneur is a testament to the importance of recognizing and nurturing individual passions and talents. His story highlights that success is not solely determined by academic performance but by dedication, resilience, and the pursuit of one's true interests. It serves as an inspiration to many average students who have unique stories and potentials waiting to be discovered and celebrated.

Finding Inspiration in Everyday Lives:

In my journey through life, I've had the privilege of meeting many individuals, each with their own unique stories. While they may have been considered average in terms of societal measures of success, each person's life narrative has been profoundly inspiring.

These encounters have shown me that greatness is not solely defined by wealth or status. The resilience, creativity, and determination of everyday people have left a lasting impact on me. Their stories, filled with personal challenges and triumphs, have demonstrated that inspiration often comes from the most unexpected places.

From humble beginnings to small victories, each individual has taught me valuable lessons about perseverance, kindness, and the human spirit. These experiences have enriched my perspective, reminding me that every life holds a story worth cherishing and learning from.

Through these connections, I've discovered that the true essence of inspiration lies not in extraordinary achievements but in the authenticity and depth of each person's journey.

In my life, the majority of people I have encountered—approximately 90% of whom were of average standing. However, they have inspired me far more than the remaining 10% who were considered exceptional.

"Every person you meet has a story to tell. The key is to listen and understand how their story matters in the larger tapestry of life. - **Satyam Tyagi"**

Forging your path forward means actively shaping your future through deliberate choices and actions. It involves taking ownership of your journey, setting clear goals, and navigating challenges with resilience. By embracing this proactive approach, you carve out a direction that aligns with your values and aspirations, ultimately leading to personal and professional growth.

Embrace Your Journey: *Encouraging individuals to embrace their unique journey and the lessons it brings.*

Discover Your Strengths: *Inspiring individuals to discover and harness their strengths for personal growth.*

Create Meaningful Connections: *Fostering meaningful connections with others and the world around them.*

Believe in Possibilities: *Encouraging individuals to believe in the endless possibilities.*

Empowering Futures: Providing Education to Underprivileged Children

It refers to initiatives or actions to provide educational opportunities to underprivileged children. This effort typically involves identifying disadvantaged children, often from low-income families or marginalized communities, and supporting them with access to schooling, educational resources, and mentorship. The goal is to break the cycle of poverty by empowering these children through education, enabling them to build a better future for themselves and their communities. Such initiatives play a crucial role in fostering equal opportunity and societal development.

Say No to Dowry: Rejecting Outdated Demands for a Modern Future

Rejecting dowry or insisting on receiving it is unjustified. If someone truly wants to be with you, their presence should be more valuable than any material demands. Building a future together should be based on mutual respect and companionship, not on financial transactions or demands from parents. Such beliefs promote equality, respect, and the foundation of a healthy relationship.

Some families of prospective grooms say they don't want a dowry, but if they desire it, they ask for their daughter. This stance is also incorrect because if she will live with you, then why ask for it from her parents?

The Reality of Friendships: Understanding Their Fragility Over Time

Continuously insulting a friend can have lasting effects on their self-esteem and the friendship itself. Over time, such remarks can erode trust and create distance between even the closest of friends. It's crucial to communicate with kindness and empathy, understanding that words have a profound impact. Building a supportive and respectful environment within friendships nurtures trust and fosters long-lasting connections. It may sound awkward to hear, but the reality is that friendships can end over time.

Empowering the Future: Taking Action for the Next Generation

Doing something meaningful for the next generation ensures a legacy of progress and prosperity. Whether through education, innovation, or social initiatives, investing in future generations empowers them to thrive and contribute positively to society. It's a noble pursuit that fosters sustainable development and creates a better world for those who follow.

Cherishing Moments: Prioritizing Time with Family and Children

Allocate quality time to family and children, as parents should never feel bored when spending time with them. These moments are precious for bonding, nurturing relationships, and creating lasting memories that shape a strong and supportive family dynamic. Active engagement fosters a sense of security, love, and understanding, laying the foundation for a harmonious and fulfilling family life. Some people think they are repaying their parents' kindness by giving them money, but you will never truly repay their kindness that way. Instead, if you just make an effort to talk to them daily and try to spend time with them, that's enough for them. They will never feel bored if you do that for them.

The Importance of Conserving Resources:

Water and food are essential resources that should not be taken for granted. It's crucial to conserve water by turning it off whenever you see it being wasted. Similarly, avoid wasting food, as it is a valuable resource that many people around the world lack. By being mindful of our consumption and waste, we contribute to a more sustainable and equitable world.

The Reality of Food Insecurity:

Many people in the world struggle to get enough food to eat. Some are so desperate that they resort to searching through dumpsters to find something edible. This reality should remind us never to waste food. Instead, we should appreciate what we have and look for ways to help those in need. By reducing food waste and sharing with others, we can make a significant difference in the lives of those less fortunate.

Maintaining Healthy Relationships:

It's important to maintain good relationships with everyone around you. If you have issues with someone at home, try to resolve them through open communication and understanding. A little argument can lead to a solution and strengthen your bond. On the other hand, if you face problems with people outside your home, it's often best to smile and ignore minor conflicts. By doing so, you can preserve your peace of mind and focus on more important matters.

www.ingramcontent.com/pod-product-compliance
Lightning Source LLC
Chambersburg PA
CBHW031142130726
47988CB00006B/2489